READY, AIM, FIRE!

CHARACTER ASSASSINATION IN CUBA

D0890656

READY, AIM, FIRE!

CHARACTER ASSASSINATION IN CUBA

Preface by Ramón Guillermo Aveledo

Rafael Rojas / Uva de Aragón
Juan Antonio Blanco / Ana Julia Faya
Carlos Alberto Montaner / Gordiano Lupi

Published by Eriginal Books LLC
Miami, Florida
www.eriginalbooks.com
www.eriginalbooks.net

Cover Design, Eduardo Elizalde
English translation, Magdalena Menocal
Style Editor, Elena Blanco Moleón

First published by Eriginal Books, May 2011
Original Title: *El otro paredón. Asesinatos de la reputación en Cuba*

ISBN-13: 978-1-61370-974-0
Library of Congress Control Number: 2012948447

Contents

Prologue to the Second Edition: 9
Continuous Homicide
Ramón Guillermo Aveledo

Prologue: 13
Character Assassinations
luan Antonio Blanco

Legitimacy and History in Cuba   35
Rafael Rojas

The Execution of Reputations: 51
Republican Politics. Carlos Márquez
Sterling and the 1958 Elections
Uva de Aragón

The Character Assassination of Cuban   75
Businessmen. An Analysis of the
Smear Campaigns against
Amadeo Barletta
Juan Antonio Blanco

An Account of Harassment and   157
Demonization
Ana Julia Faya

The How and Why of the Attempted   173
Assassination of my Reputation
Carlos Alberto Montaner

Ready, Aim, Fire... in Italy   197
Gordiano Lupi

About the authors   231

Index   241

PROLOGUE TO THE SECOND EDITION
CONTINUOUS HOMICIDE

At the end of a walk in December 1974, the Muscovite snow crunching beneath every step, we entered the Museum of the Revolution, my body grateful for the refuge from the freezing weather and to be rid of the weight of my coat, scarf, and ushanka. With the help of our interpreter, an expert at watering down any expression, the guide led us on a tour of paintings, photographs, and other mementos. After some time, I was unable to resist the temptation to ask about Trotsky as I didn't see him anywhere. The reply was yes, he was sure to be in one or another of the images, and when I asked to be shown which ones, since I had been looking carefully, the reply was that, in point of fact, the West had greatly exaggerated Trotsky's role in the Revolution. When in 1976 José Rodríguez Iturbe posed a similar question at the Smolny Institute in what was then Leningrad, the reply was: "If he isn't there, he wasn't there."

More than thirty years later, in *The Man Who Loved Dogs* (*El hombre que amaba los perros*), the powerful novel in which Padura relates how Stalin persecuted Lev Davidovich, "as the deceitful cat plays with the wretched mouse," I found the answer to another question that had long been nagging at me: Why didn't he kill him at once? The truth is that Stalin kept him alive long enough to use him as a pretext for killing many others, and by the time he finally got rid of him, he had already been killing him bit by bit, inasmuch as his propaganda machine had been tearing his reputation to shreds. From the hero he had once been, Trotsky was described as a "left-deviationist", traitor, enemy; he was expelled from the USSR in 1929, deprived of Soviet citizenship in 1932, and harassed in Turkey, France, Norway, and Mexico, where he was finally murdered in 1940.

One could cynically allege that for the Bolshevik Revolution's military chief it was a case of assassination pure and simple rather than character assassination, but as the aforementioned Rodríguez Iturbe indicates[1]: "The point was not merely to turn opponents into the "living dead" (political death, social irrelevance, total marginalization, absolute exclusion), but for them to be "dead-dead" (that is, dead in the literal sense of the word, as a result of the loss of life)".

---

[1] Rodríguez Iturbe, José: *Trotsky y el trotskismo original. Las persecución del fundamentalismo stalinista.* University of Sabana-Temis. Bogotá, 2010.

Character assassination—the destruction of an individual's or a social group's reputation—is practiced by régimes or political movements with totalitarian inclinations. Stalin died, but this practice continued to be used against dissidents in the defunct Soviet Union. Aleksandr Solzhenitsyn, who had been expelled from the Union of Soviet Writers in 1969, was stripped of his citizenship after the publication of *The Gulag Archipelago* in Paris. Jews, collectively, were systematically discredited under the Third Reich, during which the cinema, especially in 1940 and 1941, served to legitimize the State's anti-Semite war to the point where merely uttering the word Jew was an insult. Doctor Goebbels's mass propaganda was also used to turn popular culture, to such an extent that the Nazi revolution thereafter became the definitive break with the country's political past. Others who were publicly and consistently insulted were the communists, the socialists, and Catholic and Protestant priests and activists. The trial of the Jesuit Delp in January 1945 was compared to the medieval witch trials by the presiding judge Freisler himself, who at the height of the trial described Delp as "a rat...he should be squashed underfoot". Rats, too, is what Colonel Gadaffi called his opponents; under Castro, as under Hitler before him, they were called worms, and cockroaches by Sierra Leone's military dictatorships in the nineties.

At an individual level, the accusation can consist of one or several epithets: traitor, thief, murderer, corrupt individual, pervert, foreign agent. These exaggerations, half-truths, manipulation of facts, or else outright slander are repeated with the confidence afforded by impunity, and from a position of power that guarantees that the person in question will never be granted an equal opportunity to respond. During the Trujillo era in the Dominican Republic, the items in the Public Forum section of *El Caribe* newspaper were feared. Time and time again, mass media has been used for the purpose of character assassination, and not only in the case of well-known tyrannical régimes or those universally recognized as such. In Peru under Fujimori, who divested Mario Vargas Llosa of his Peruvian nationality, tabloid journalism was encouraged, as were radio and television broadcasts under the direction of the sinister Vladimir Lenin Montesinos. In Chávez's Venezuela, expert at imitating the bad habits of other countries, in addition to the presidential channels on all television and radio networks, the propaganda bombardment occurs on any day, at any time, and for any reason via the Public Media System's television and radio broadcasting stations, the print media, and through a fairly efficient use of so-called social networks, used to disseminate rumors and disinformation.

During my years as a student, I remember the description of "continuous theft" in criminal law courses, the typical example of which was the housemaid who steals her mistress' necklace pearl by pearl. If that's the case, then character assassination would be a form of continuous homicide. A progressive and, going back to the logic of criminal law, motivated tearing-to-pieces since, being carefully planned and executed. It is committed with premeditation; with malice, given that those committing it run no risk whatsoever and instead gain benefits and privileges; and with advantage, since the acts are carried out from a position of power, all of which make such despicable activities even viler.

This book, whose 2011 first edition I avidly read, is about character assassination. An interesting essay by the Italian writer Gordiano Lupi has been added to the already fascinating pieces by Rafael Rojas, Uva de Aragón, Juan Antonio Blanco, Ana Julia Faya and Carlos Alberto Montaner. In gratitude for the literary nourishment provided by the first edition, I write these lines to introduce the second edition of *Ready, Aim, Fire! Character Assassination in Cuba*, a subject matter that, to our shame, is still a topical one in our countries.

Ramón Guillermo Aveledo
Caracas, April 2012

PROLOGUE
CHARACTER ASSASSINATIONS

Many people consider their reputations to be something worth valuing above life itself. Throughout history, there has been no shortage of individuals who have fought duels to the death over matters of honor. Quite a few nations have gone to war with others or annihilated entire segments of their population purportedly in defense of their national honor or that of their race.

Character assassination is a deliberate and sustained process that aims to destroy the credibility and reputation of a person, institution, social group, or nation.

Agents of character assassinations employ a mix of open and covert methods to achieve their goals, such as raising false accusations, planting and fostering rumors, and manipulating information.

The most common purposes of character assassinations are to ultimately nullify the victims' potential for influencing others, silence their voices, and promote their rejection from society. By transforming its victims into non-persons, they also make them vulnerable to even greater abuses like physical aggression, incarceration, confiscation of properties, expatriation, murder, and even genocide of the social group to which they belong.

The Nazis' anti-Semitic propaganda and the Holocaust that followed are extreme examples of the dangers related to state-sponsored character assassination campaigns. When a government resorts to this approach when it needs to justify aggressions and abuses against its victims, it can be considered to represent a form of state terrorism. As a general rule, mass murders, crimes against humanity, and genocides tend to be preceded by a campaign of this nature.

With the arrival of the Web 2.0 and virtual social networks in the 21st Century, the dissemination of falsehoods can now be implemented in a swifter and much more efficient fashion. The seeds of prejudices planted against the victims gradually take root in the social collective memory, and common people – particularly the new generations– accept them as true history and real biographies.

As time goes on, the false perceptions that were deliberately fabricated and disseminated through various means of communications can eventually infiltrate educational systems and become the official, socially accepted history. By the time the fabricated prejudices reach this point, they are quite difficult to revert.

When the real history of a person is erased from collective memory and replaced by a counterfeited image that others are meant to fear or reject, the offense equates with the literal murder of a human life. Except the damage caused by this symbolic form of assassination can be drawn out indefinitely.

What are the implications of deliberately assassinating a person's character, or of ruining a social group's or institution's reputation? What might be the implications of such actions if they are occurring as a response to the initiatives of a government with sufficient resources to exercise this kind of state-sponsored terrorism? *Ready, Aim, Fire! Character Assassination in Cuba* analyzes this topic through the lens of the Cuban experience over the last fifty years.

Why venture into the subject of state-sponsored character assassinations fostered by the Cuban government now? Why talk about Cuba in particular and not about what is occurring elsewhere in regards to this subject?

The reason is simply that Cuban society is bound to approach a critical juncture in its development. It seems inevitable that, one way or another, different processes leading to social change will occur on the island, although we should bear in mind that such change does not always happen quickly and conclusively. Experience has taught us that closed societies are sometimes able to quickly change symbolic facets of the social order that are superficial in nature, but that the old régime lives on in more deeply ingrained structures—mindsets, prejudices, concepts—that remain embedded in the subconscious mind, and even in that of their opponents.

The reunification of the Cuban nation requires not just bringing an end to the laws of banishment and establishing a democratic rule of law on the island, but also presupposes the eradication of the prejudices that have kept its society divided. Nation-wide reconciliation cannot fully take place so long as there are a significant number of people who, even if they do not sympathize with the current régime, continue to assume that the victims got into trouble "because they asked for it", that those who left lost all of their rights because they "deserted their country", or that those who pursue private enterprise or political activities do so "because they are opportunists or power hungry".

The following articles and short essays provide the reader with an overview of the deliberate ways in which, for half a century, the Cuban government has constructed mindsets that in the name of social justice and nationalism have in fact paved the way for the wielding of absolute power by an elite class. For fifty years, an extensive mechanism, which encompasses propaganda, and cultural and educational systems, has been in operation, fostering social biases against all those who, either from the left or the right, have not allied themselves with the elite's interests and objectives.

The character assassinations described in this book are not equivalent to those that can be carried out by a political party against the government, or by a dissatisfied consumer group against a restaurant. We are not talking about personal defamation or institutional criticism. We are talking about an organized form of state-sponsored terrorism aimed at the deliberate and total destruction of the credibility of a person, group, or institution.

In the now defunct Soviet Union, the KGB was responsible for designing and executing smear campaigns against people classified as "anti-Soviet". One of the many objectives would be the destruction of a foreign politician's credibility, or the questioning of a well-known dissident's motives and personal integrity, or creating doubts as to the sincerity of an individual who defected with valuable information, whom it later became necessary to discredit in order for him or her to be given short shrift.

The compilation of documents from KGB files published by Christopher Andrew and Vasili Mitrokhin (*The Mitrokhin Archive*, 1999, pp. 421-422) contains a long list of guidelines personally provided on November 22, 1975 by then KGB director Yuri Andropov for challenging the awarding of the Nobel Peace Prize to Andrei Sakharov. The KGB showed itself to have absolutely no scruples in its activities, which included distributing a supposedly congratulatory telegram sent to the scientist by the Chilean dictator Augusto Pinochet and fabricating stories about his wife that portrayed her as an opportunist who seduced older men of influence for her personal benefit.

Among the many instructions given to hundreds of KGB officers (whether they were acting under the guise of diplomats or simply undercover), and to the networks of agents under their command, there included orders for finding a way to spread rumors in the press, on radio and television programs, and in cultural, scientific, political, and diplomatic media outlets. As stated by Andrew and Mitrokhin in their book (p. 632), in the late eighties the KGB's ability to access leading Western media outlets was significantly diminished.

Cuba learned its most advanced character assassination techniques from its "socialist brothers". In order to apply them, a systematic mechanism was constructed within the Ministry of the Interior specifically devoted to conceiving these types of activities and coordinating them with the various civil agencies within the Cuban Communist Party and the government.

With the advent of the Web 2.0, the Cuban government discovered the Internet's potential as a tool in character assassination campaigns and for implanting more "active measures". In the era of global communications, it is no longer essential to woo journalists, editors, or filmmakers. One need only put together a network of like-minded opinion leaders to create blogs, post comments onto online articles published by the leading media, or upload documentaries to YouTube. The new programs for digitally processing text and images also eliminate the need for a large group of specialists to falsify documents and photographs. Character assassination now uses viral marketing techniques. With a group of voluntary cybercops operating from within Cuba and their respective collaborators abroad, it becomes possible to multiply the links which lead to negative messages about this or that individual "planted" by the state propaganda machine at various junctions throughout the World Wide Web.

In Cuba, the design of these online character assassinations often takes the form of concentric circles of disinformation artificially constructed to spread a message fabricated by the propaganda machine, which disseminates it on the Internet, like a virtual snowball. In order to launch the initial defamation, one need only choose a national writer willing to "cooperate" in this task, and ask him or her to publish a book or an article. This messenger is then given a boost by the local media, and one or two official institutions present him or her with a cultural, journalistic, or academic award. These steps build the character assassination's initial and still-local circle. Later, a second circle is constructed to export the message via "solidarity" foreign nationals living outside of Cuba, in an attempt to give a certain amount of credibility to the original accusation. The success of these operations begins when people or media without any known form of sympathy for the Cuban government inadvertently pick up the message under the mistaken assumption that, with so many sources backing it up, there is no need to confirm its truthfulness or origin.

One could think, and rightfully so, that denigrating a political opponent is, after all, a fairly widespread practice among the world's biggest democracies; but the effect of a smear campaign driven by an individual is not equal to that of a state-driven campaign.

The state-sponsored destruction of reputations, fostered by political propaganda and cultural mechanisms, can have more far-reaching consequences. How was the cooperation of the masses with crimes against humanity and genocide gained in societies as diverse as Germany and Rwanda? How did the atrocities of the Cultural Revolution in China or the genocide in Cambodia become feasible?

One of the earliest signs of a society's compliance to loosening the reins on the perpetration of crimes (and even massacres) with total impunity is when a government favors or directly encourages a campaign aimed at destroying the dignity and reputation of its adversaries, and the public accepts its allegations without question. The mobilization toward ruining the reputation of adversaries is the prelude to the mobilization of violence in order to annihilate them. Official dehumanization has always preceded the physical assault of the victims.

When decent people begin taking part in carrying out indecent actions, or showing indifference to them, a widespread ethical deterioration begins. Those in power disseminate an official morality that negates universal ethical values. Under the new moral canon, the giving of a collective beating to an unarmed "enemy" turns an act of cowardice into a virtue. The "new man" is, above all, defined by his acceptance of the principle of unconditional obedience to authority. The willingness to die for a cause is, above all, the willingness to kill one's fellow man should the leader order it so.

Although in some places dissidents are called a variety of insults such as "roaches" (Sierra Leone), in others "rats" (Libya), or "worms" (Nazi Germany, Cuba), the common denominator in these societies is the presence of leaders whose wisdom cannot be questioned. They free the masses from any sense of guilt when called upon to inflict physical or psychological abuse, torture, or even death upon another human being.

This is why we need to take note that in the case of the Cuban government, the justification for each act of cruelty has been embellished with pejorative adjectives for the victims. Orlando Zapata Tamayo, who died in prison as a result of a prolonged hunger strike protesting the inhumanity with which he was treated by his jailers, was undeserving of any pity because he was an alleged "criminal". The dissident Guillermo Fariñas, who through another hunger strike called upon the government to free political prisoners in poor health, was undeserving of the Sakharov Prize awarded by the European Parliament because he was another alleged "criminal". The Ladies in White (*Damas de Blanco*), who march along Cuba's streets carrying flowers and demanding the release of jailed family members, are "mercenaries"; hence, there is no reason to blush should a mob surround and insult them for hours on end, or even physically attack any of them. Political exiles are "gangsters" and therefore are not entitled to return to live in their country nor so much as enter it freely. Those who rejected Cuban socialism and left en masse via the port of El Mariel are called "scum". The bloggers and freelance journalists who write about the harsh reality of Cuban society are "provocateurs who facilitate foreign military intervention".

This extreme political rhetoric is endorsed through the creation of "active measures" against dissidents — rumors, falsified documents, agents infiltrated among opponents who encourage opposition members to commit acts that enable them to be legally charged or discredited, and other similar ruses. In this way, people or institutions who may not even sympathize with the Cuban régime unconsciously come to accept its basic assumptions in the same way that other people were previously led to believe that Pinochet was Sakharov's friend.

One important instance is the character assassination of the so-called "Marielitos".

After two decades of socialism, Fidel Castro attempted to obscure the failure of the new régime implied by the mass exodus of some 125,000 Cubans through the port of El Mariel. On the boats picking up the potential migrants, the Cuban leader mingled individuals with criminal records and common prisoners with regular people and families, and accused them all of being scum and criminals. But the myth that honest individuals—who subsequently demonstrated their honesty and industriousness —constituted a threat to the public safety of the United States was only able to take root when Hollywood produced a popular remake of *Scarface* with a prominent artist like Al Pacino. The violent character he portrayed, Tony Montana, became, in the public's imagination, the representation of every "Marielito". With *Scarface*, Hollywood unintentionally crowned the work begun by the Cuban government against those who chose to leave via El Mariel.

The road to national reconciliation will be much more difficult and steep if we do not question the myths of hate propaganda and lay bare state-sponsored character assassinations. This book is therefore as timely and relevant as the initiative by the two universities that prompted its publication. On November 15, 2010, the International Institute of Juridical Studies (IEJI as per its initials in Spanish) of Madrid's Rey Juan Carlos University and the Cuban Research Institute at Florida International University organized an event on Historiography and Politics analyzing how certain facts, individuals, and social groups were treated in official chronicles of Cuban history as of 1959. The present compilation gathers and expands on the analyses by three speakers at that event: Rafael Rojas, Uva de Aragón, and the writer of this prologue.

Rafael Rojas, a prominent intellectual and his generation's most outstanding historian on Cuban theory, centers his analysis on how, from the very beginning, the Cuban régime has coordinated a deliberate attempt to construct an official history that would contribute to its legitimization. In this pursuit, it has never hesitated in blotting out or destroying the reputation of any person or anything considered inconvenient to maintaining the official version.

As this eminent Cuban intellectual says: "Official history therefore stems from an ideological and moral selection of past players, wherein those who make up the power bloodline are remembered, and those who were not a part of it fade into oblivion. To a large extent, such an account functions as a court of final judgment that decides the fate of historical subjects, and consigns them to either hell or paradise, remembrance or oblivion."

Uva de Aragón, a highly-regarded writer on the historical Cuban exile, for whom the absence of hate and support for reconciliation has been a constant philosophy, analyzes the way in which the prerevolutionary political class was demonized, even prior to 1959, and the arbitrariness with which the reputations of its members—including that of her step-father, Carlos Márquez Sterling, who honorably and with great fairness presided over the Constituent Assembly of 1940—

were attacked with all the force and resources of the revolutionary government.

Márquez Sterling earned the personal enmity of Fidel Castro early on when he tried, up to the last possible moment, to find a political solution to the crisis of 1958. He believed in votes, not bullets, which is why Castro's 26th of July Movement attempted more than once to assassinate him. From 1959 onwards and without a single shred of evidence, official Cuban history has insisted on besmirching a man who died, humble and respected, in exile.

The analysis regarding the entrepreneur Amadeo Barletta shows how the Cuban government also relied on character assassination to justify confiscating the assets of businessmen who did not make their fortunes during Batista's tenure, and later, beginning in 1989, to counteract the scandals resulting from the drug trafficking operations involving Cuban military structures.

The rigorous scrutiny of numerous original documental sources confirms the falsehood of the arguments used by the campaigns against this successful Italian immigrant, whose vision and industriousness enabled him to rebuild his businesses after they were seriously affected on five separate occasions – due to the destructive forces of a natural disaster, three dictators, and a civil war.

Two additional authors, Ana Julia Faya and Carlos Alberto Montaner, illustrate the manner in which, although they come from opposite intellectual traditions—Marxist and liberal—both of them have been plagued by the type of state-sponsored terrorism that is character assassination.

Faya, merely by being a member of the University of Havana's Philosophy Department, was accused, along with the department's entire faculty, of being an either conscious or unconscious member of the CIA, of ideological divergence, and of other nasty offenses by Raúl Castro – charges that in the Cuba of 1971 could result in imprisonment and severe suppression. The story repeated itself at the Center for American Studies (*Centro de Estudios de América*, CEA), of which Faya was a member – all of whom were accused, in 1996, again by Raúl Castro, of ideological crimes similar to those imputed to the university's philosophy professors in 1971.

In a letter to Fidel and Raúl Castro, Ana Julia Faya demanded a public apology to the CEA's academicians for the accusations leveled against them, none of which were ever proved; the accused have yet to receive an apology. Instead, the Ministry of Culture has attempted to erase any symbolic aspects of past campaigns. While this is not necessarily a bad thing, as long as there is no public acknowledgement of the way in which those affronts were actually cooked up and carried out, and the circumstances that made them possible have not been eradicated, the same threat will continue to loom over new victims.

Faya's case shows that although many, such as Montaner, have been persecuted for their liberal ideas and anticommunist militancy, others have also been persecuted—and attempts have been made to destroy their reputations—because of their unorthodox interpretation of socialism and Marxism.

The case of Carlos Alberto Montaner is emblematic of the topic we are dealing with here. With singular obsession and determination, an extraordinary stockpile of the most varied accusations has been disseminated against him.

This prominent Cuban oppositionist politician, intellectual, and writer has, in pro-Castro mythology, been turned into something akin to the black monolith representing Satan at Mecca, an icon toward which every good follower of Islam must make a pilgrimage at least once in his lifetime in order to hurl stones at it. The demand that is made of the "good revolutionary" is not that he must rationally disagree with Montaner, which one is nonetheless entitled and encouraged to do, so as to contribute towards enriching their audience's viewpoint, but that he thoroughly hate, accuse, insult, and abuse the man.

One day he might be accused of murdering left-leaning priests, another day of being the reason for the continued existence of the U.S. embargo, yet another of being responsible for the awarding of international prizes to the Cuban blogger Yoani Sánchez, and very soon he will also be blamed for the latest drought to hit the island. The main objective of the campaign against Montaner, which mirrors that which was pursued by the KGB against the most prominent Soviet dissidents, is nothing less than to discredit and isolate him in an attempt to counteract his international influence.

Regrettably, there still exists a sector of the Left whose ingenuousness and ideological bigotry turns it into a natural collaborator of professional character assassins. These are the sort of people who, should they come into power, will persecute Montaner just as viciously as they would persecute those within their own ranks who dare to dissent, as was the case with Ana Julia Faya in Cuba. In their eyes, Montaner's defense of liberal democracy and the market is crime enough to accept *prima facie* any accusation against him, and Faya's ideological insubordination equals apostasy. The murder of the poet Roque Dalton, also accused of being a CIA agent by those who considered him a nuisance, is just one example of where that road leads.

Marxist poets and academicians are being accused of acting as either conscious or unconscious agents for the CIA, and Montaner is accused of belonging to the agency itself. The reality is that the accusers have never been overly concerned with proving one theory or the other; they don't really care about that. In totalitarian countries, it is not the public prosecutors who must prove the guilt of the accused, but rather the latter who must—generally to no avail—try to prove their innocence. In any case, after half a century of hurling that accusation against numerous highly regarded individuals—as was done in the sixties to figures such as K. S. Karol and Oscar Lewis—the argument has been losing its persuasive effectiveness.

The bad news is that after a half century the Cuban leaders insist in assassinating the reputation of those who dissent from their regime. Their fantastic accusations should not be taken lightly. Cuba's official media —and a sector of the international left that is always ready to extend its unconditional support to a regime that claims to be "socialist" — accuses the Cuban independent bloggers and journalists of being mercenaries. Without so much as a red flush on their faces they say that with their articles they are deliberately working to provide justification for a foreign military intervention. That's no small accusation in a country where the death penalty is prescribed for crimes of that nature and legal due process is notoriously absent.

When that extravagant Left, who reside far from their imagined paradises, lend themselves to spreading defamations against the celebrated Cuban blogger Yoani Sanchez and her colleagues, they become complicit –and responsible– for what may befall them. The Italian journalist Gordiano Lupi delves into that story in this expanded edition of Ready, Aim, Fire.

Additionally, as a reminder that the Cuban regime has exported not only doctors to Venezuela, but also experts in implementing "active measures" to assassinate political dissidents in honor of the South American country, the distinguished academic Ramón Guillermo Aveledo has also written the foreword to this new edition. Cubans are not the only ones who must face this challenge.

The good news is that the era of character assassination is coming to an end despite the multiple biases embedded within Cuban society. What is truly new and encouraging in Cuba is not the government and its occasional political turnabouts, but the change that is occurring in the attitudes of the island's population. Young adults no longer blindly accept the official versions of history regarding people and facts. They want to find out the truth of what actually happened during all these idealized past decades. The Cuban people, including active party members and officials, are beginning to lose their fear of talking.

And there will be a great deal to talk about and to fathom.

Knowing exactly what happened and why becomes a necessity. The facts must be put into context in order to better understand why each person took the path he or she did throughout this lengthy conflict.

Those of us who thought we were contributing to a better society suddenly find ourselves having contributed to erecting a régime without basic freedoms that ended up destroying the sources of national wealth and spreading poverty around; we must explain the reasoning behind our mindsets. And those who, in opposing the repression of the Cuban government, violated the human rights of those who sympathized with the Revolution or of others they made victims who were not even a part of this conflict, must also do the same.

The future reconciliation between Cubans demands this contextualized understanding of past perceptions and actions. We must learn from our republican and post-republican history so as to identify the "never agains" into which we must not fall trap in the future. Neither blowing up a passenger plane nor sinking a ship crammed with undocumented migrant families are justifiable acts.

Today, Cuban economists argue about the best options for reconstructing the country's material viability. Historians will have to reconstruct the facts as they occurred, even if they subsequently differ on how to interpret them. That shall be their contribution to the reconstruction of the island's future. Besides being a professional responsibility, there is another virtuous reason for doing it: it is their ethical duty towards the many victims whose assaulted dignity await reaffirmation.

It is difficult to know where we should be headed when we don't yet know where we're coming from.

Juan Antonio Blanco
April 2011

LEGITIMACY AND HISTORY IN CUBA

Rafael Rojas

Modernist thinkers on the right, such as Hans Kelsen and Herbert L. A. Hart, acknowledged by liberals or Marxists as theoretical sources, posited the legal dilemma of revolutions as a two-part movement: the fracture of the previous legitimacy and the creation of the new one. In the period during which the preceding State is destroyed and the new one is created, both concepts of legitimacy enter into a binary conflict in which each portrays the other as illegitimate. However, there always comes a time when a new constitution is established and "the acts that arise in the subjective sense from producing and applying legal norms are now construed by presupposing not the old basic norm, but the new one".[2]

This process of legal conflict has been evident in all revolutions —the English, American, French, or Mexican—but is more intense and intermittent in the

---

[2] Hans Kelsen, *Teoría pura del derecho*, Mexico City, UNAM, 1979, p. 219. See also H. L. A. Hart, *El concepto del Derecho*, Buenos Aires, Abeledo-Perrot, 1968, p. 103.

case of revolutions like the Russian, Chinese, or Cuban where the transit towards the new legitimacy occurs beyond the paradigm of the modern liberal state. In these latter communist revolutions, the enactment and application of the new constitution that will confer legitimacy on the new political players must use centralized, plebiscitary, charismatic, or limited forms of political representation, wherein what is legitimate is confined to the state and insisted upon before a group of illegitimate subjects encompassed under labels such as "counterrevolutionaries", "enemies of the people" or "traitors to the country".

The legal philosopher Ulises Schmill summarizes the difference between the processes for building legitimacy used by both revolutionary varieties—liberal and communist—with the concept that in the latter, unlike the former, the new legitimacy always incorporates a parallel symbolic fabrication of the opposition's illegitimacy.[3] This functional vision of antagonism, similar to that described by Carl Schmitt in his *Teoría del partisano* (Theory of the Partisan, 1985), intensifies the legitimizing process, and places demands on it for symbolic affirmation that differ from those of a liberal or democratic state. By taking the coercive legal prem-

---

[3] Ulises Schmill, *Las revoluciones. Teoría jurídica y consideraciones sociológicas*, Madrid, Trotta, 2009, pp.17-19.

ise to its logical conclusion, the revolutionary order generates, in a manner of speaking, a more intense longing for legitimization, inscribing its institutional framework in the consolidation of stasis rather than the representation of demos.[4]

Stasis was the concept used by the Greeks to designate a state of civil war in the polis and is articulated in Thucydides' History of the Peloponnesian War.[5] Schmill maintains that revolutionary legitimacy is a symbolic continuation of civil war via the new state's institutions. The principle of belligerence that serves as its bedrock demands, as we said, a more elaborate and insistent ideological cover than does the democratic order. One element of that cover, precisely since Thucydides, is a community's history, that is, a chronicle of the founding and evolution of the polis in accordance with the symbols of the power established.

Every political régime and every government, democratic or not, resorts to an official history in order to legitimize itself. This history is a result of the processing of historiographic consensuses by a country's political, educational, and media institutions in the public domain. In democracies, the possibilities of challenging official narratives are naturally greater than

---

[4] Ibid, pp. 74-76.
[5] Ibid, pp. 56-57.

under authoritarian or totalitarian régimes because freedom of speech and the legal autonomy of cultural institutions expand the dissemination of historical discourse and limit the construction of hegemonic accounts. The global weakening of national ideologies over the last two decades as a consequence of the end of the Cold War makes the intellectual market more competitive and, therefore, the construction of hegemonic recollections more contested.

Even in a country like Cuba, where a nondemocratic political system has persisted for over half a century, a few symptoms of that ideological weakening can be detected despite the still considerable longing for symbolic legitimization. Over the last twenty years, also in Cuba, the public discourse has been disseminated, and in the case of the production and circulation of historical knowledge, that increasing dissemination is reflected in academic historiography's greater independence, in respect for the official history, and in a more inclusive and less teleological portrayal of players from the past in social science publications. The official story has not disappeared as a component of the legitimizing apparatus, but its sphere of influence in terms of the press, radio, and television is gradually diminishing and it is losing its reproductive capacity in higher education and intellectual circles.[6]

Quite symptomatic of the weakening of the Cuban régime's mechanisms for historical legitimization is their increasing limitation not just to *Granma*, *Juventud Rebelde*, National Television or the State Council's publishing press, but to Fidel Castro's circle of personal associates. Whereas academic historians have relaunched one of the old régime's institutions—the Academy of History of Cuba—and insist, with or without ambivalence, that it be endowed with the "traditional" or inorganic concept of "autonomy", the official discourse's historical partisanship finds reinforcement in the symbolic center of power: the person of Fidel Castro. The recent books *La victoria estratégica* (Strategic Victory, 2010) and *La contraofensiva estratégica* (Strategic Counteroffensive, 2010), written by Castro himself, in collaboration with historical advisors such as Pedro Álvarez Tabío, Rolando Rodríguez, and Katiushka Blanco, and edited by the Council of State, are a testament to the ever more precarious survival of Cuba's official history.

The survival is precarious because of the continually decreasing receptiveness to this account within

---

[6] Rafael Rojas, "El debate historiográfico y las reglas del campo intelectual en Cuba", in Araceli Tinajero, *Cultura y letras cubanas en el siglo XXI*, Madrid, Iberoamericana/Vervuert, 2010, pp. 131-146.

academic and intellectual circles, which until recently were its principal means of communication; but it survives nonetheless, inasmuch as these books, just like the still recent *Biografía a dos voces* (Biography in Two Voices, 2006) by Ignacio Ramonet, as well as those "reflections" dealing with historical topics, contain Cuba's official history in a nutshell and are published and subsidized to the tune of hundreds of thousands of copies and reproduced in the principal mass media. The extraordinary circulation rate attained by these documents is sufficient to confirm their proselytizing and educational role, their functionality in ideologically constituting or preserving a loyal citizenry and, hence, in consolidating legitimacy by means of narrative. This official literature is the best evidence that in Cuba, in contrast to any democracy, the Constitution and legislation are not enough to guarantee legitimacy, which must be continually fed by a hegemonic account of the past that justifies the lack of freedom in the present.

This account, such as it appears in text, could be summarized as follows: Cuba was a Spanish colony from 1492 to 1898 when it became a colony of the United States. In the 19th century, Cubans strove for independence, and that century's most comprehensive national project, devised by José Martí, contemplated not just independence from Spain, but also from the United States since the Apostle warned that the island's sovereignty would pass from hand to hand between Madrid and Washington should his revolution not be victorious. The intervention by the United States in 1898 thwarted that national project, which certain leaders of the 1920s and 1930s tried to revive, men like the communist Julio Antonio Mella and the socialist Antonio Guiteras, that lineage's two most senior politicians from the first half of the 20th century.[7] This revolution, which attempted to revive Martí's project, also failed thanks to the United States, the island's oligarchy, and authoritarian or corrupt politicians such as Fulgencio Batista, Ramón Grau San Martín, and Carlos Prío Socarrás.

Just as 19th century separatists had to struggle, not just against Spain and the United States, but also against non-revolutionary "reformist, autonomist and annexationist movements", these leaders of the twenties and thirties had to struggle against imperialism, Machado's dictatorship, the oligarchy, and the "pseudo-revolutionaries".[8] The latter would include, between 1940 and 1958, almost every anti-Machado politician with a liberal and democratic ideology who formed a government or represented the opposition

---

[7] Ignacio Ramonet, *Fidel Castro. Biografía a dos voces*, Barcelona, debate, 2006, pp. 65-78.

[8] *Ibid*, p.29.

under the presidencies of Grau, Prío, and Batista. In *Biography in Two Voices*, an exception is made for Eduardo Chibás, who personifies the struggle against corruption within the limits of bourgeois democracy, but in the most recent introduction to *Strategic Victory* (2010), the judgment of that generation is categorical:

> *Cuba was not an independent country in 1953. Martí's ideas had been betrayed by the Republic's politicians. Most of the anti-Machado or anti-Batista revolutionaries of the thirties had become pseudo-revolutionaries. The only party with a revolutionary vision was the communist party, but it was isolated. Hence, it was essential to launch a revolutionary program outside that party to win over the majority of the population and then lead a revolutionary change through socialism.*[9]

All these writings reiterate the official history's symbolic nucleus, which is nothing less than the fantasy that Cuba has had only one revolution, which broke out in October 1868 and, after several disappointments, triumphed on January 1, 1959. Ramonet's celebrated interviewee repeated this much to him, tautologically, "October 10, 1868 is when we say—and I said so—the Revolution began".[10] *Strategic Victory* even declares that

---

[9] Fidel Castro. *La victoria estratégica,* Havana, State Council, 2010.

[10] Ignacio Ramonet, op. cit., p.32.

as of 1953 these leaders became convinced that the only way for that many-times-thwarted Revolution to triumph was through a Marxist-Leninist project: "We had to start from scratch. By the time I graduated from high-school, and despite my background, I already had a Marxist-Leninist concept of our society and a profound belief in justice."[11]

This starting-from-scratch was the only way to once again pick up the thread of a codified history that was intended to lead to socialism, except that the socialist system could not be defended openly given the intense anticommunism Washington had transmitted to the island's citizens, which lessened the prerevolutionary communist movement's popularity. The articulation of a non-communist political project in all the documents of the 26th of July Movement, in the pacts signed by the Movement with other anti-Batista opposition organizations such as the Revolutionary governing body or the Authentic Party, and in a variety of letters, articles, and statements to the national and foreign press by Fidel Castro himself, between 1953 and 1960, is presented in this reference list not as the movement's true ideological orientation, but as a picture of moderation deliberately assumed by communist leaders who

---

[11] Fidel Castro, op. cit.

were compelled to conceal their aims in order to achieve them.

An extremely revealing passage in the second book, *Strategic Counteroffensive* (2010), maintains that all those anti-Batista politicians who in one way or another opposed this undeclared socialist project between 1953 and 1960 were erased from history. A propos of Ramón Grau San Martín, of Carlos Márquez Sterling, and other orthodox or genuine leaders who participated, as opponents to Batista in the 1954 and 1958 elections, Fidel states: "Soon after Batista's defeat, in December 1958, they were forgotten by everyone. The new generations have never heard their names mentioned."[12] That the island's citizenry is not familiar with these politicians from Cuba's past is not only a bad thing, but also inevitable, since by opposing the natural course of history, they were buried by it.

Official history therefore stems from an ideological and moral selection of past players wherein those who make up the power bloodline are remembered, and those who were not a part of it fade into oblivion. To a large extent, such an account functions as a court of final judgment that decides the fate of his-

---

[12] Fidel Castro, *La contraofensiva estratégica*, Havana, State Council, 2010.

torical subjects and consigns them to either hell or paradise, remembrance or oblivion. The dissimilarities between this manner of chronicling a country's history and the academic methods used by historians could not be more marked. Very few serious historians—be they Marxist, liberal, or of any other ideological or methodological bent—would agree with classifying important figures from a nation's past as memorable or forgettable.

But beyond this incongruity, academic historians would be hard pressed to accept some of the official story's other premises, such as that of a single revolution between 1868 and 1959, of a one-and-the-same national project from José Martí through Fidel Castro, or of the absence of sovereignty between 1902 and 1959. There is no question that the Platt Amendment limited Cuban sovereignty between 1902 and 1934 (the year in which it was repealed) through Washington's right of intervention in the event of civil war, as well as in the subordination to the United States of the emerging republic's international relations. But during these three decades, the Cuban government was not entirely lacking in self-determination regarding its internal and foreign policies, a fact evidenced, for instance, during the years Manuel Sanguily was Secretary of State under President José Miguel Gómez.

The academic historical records produced within and beyond the island show that Cuba's social, economic, political, and cultural life between 1902 and 1958 was extremely intense and cannot be reduced to the context of a U.S. colony. During the early revolutionary decades, Marxist historiography tried to develop the concept of a neo-colony, which at least tempered the degree of dependence on the United States during that half century. Nonetheless, in the official history's most disseminated versions, which are those appearing in the aforementioned texts, that tempering is discarded in lieu of the precise equivalence between the prerevolutionary past and the colonial status, which denies republican political players any capacity for action.

To the Revolution's historical leaders, starting from scratch meant redesigning the national calendar to begin on a specific year zero: 1959. All that happened before that year, except that which served as a herald or prophecy, had to be referenced to the island's colonial past and therefore capitalist, bourgeois, corrupt, and "pre-national" past. The establishment of the State properly began with the Revolution, whose leaders were nothing less than the founding fathers of the "true nation". The worldwide dissemination of that premise, attained over the last century, which from a social science or political history perspective can be categorized as "false", can only be explained through a myth, which, like all myths, is not contrary to reality, but hyperbolizes one aspect of reality.

Many were the Cuban, Latin American, European, and American intellectuals who during socialism's first three decades contributed to the writing of that mythology: Jean Paul Sartre, Charles Wright Mills, Ezequiel Martínez Estrada, Eduardo Galeano, Cintio Vitier, or Roberto Fernández Retamar to name but a few. Within the island, most academic historians and political essayists (Julio Le Riverend, Jorge Ibarra, Ramón de Armas, Oscar Pino Santos, Lionel Soto, Francisco López Segrera, Pedro Pablo Rodríguez...) also participated in sustaining the fantasy of a single revolution, stigmatizing the republican period or doctrinally coupling José Martí with Marxist-Leninism. A simplified and bureaucratic version of these authors' ideas passed into the vernacular of ideologues as well as Cuban government and Communist Party leaders.

Over the past twenty years, however, that discursive schooling has gradually lost strength and sophistication. In *Biography in Two Voices*, *Strategic Victory*, and *Strategic Counteroffensive*, the official history already appears as a caricature of itself in which the personalization of Cuban history is accented by the autobiographical tone that predominates in all three books.

Fidel Castro, a leading player from the past, naturally lacks a historian's objectivity, and his opinions on Manuel Urrutia, Huber Matos, or Carlos Franqui, to name just three examples, possess a rhetorical texture that is unacceptable in academic language.[13] The new generations of aspiring official historians are, it seems, incapable of producing works equal to those of their predecessors in the sixties, seventies, and eighties and would rather turn the leader's partial memories into textbooks on the "nation's true history".[14]

One of the features of the last twenty postcommunist years is that while the official history is caricatured in the media and is eschewed in intellectual and academic circles, the opposition to the Cuban government has become mostly peaceful and has forsaken challenging the régime's illegitimacy. Most opponents, of course, believe the Cuban government to be illegitimate from a democratic point of view, but they do not challenge it as if it were a *de facto* régime that must be overthrown by force. One could say that the paradox in recent years is that whereas the government's legal legitimacy has been able to establish itself more clearly,

---

[13] Ignacio Ramonet, op. cit., pp. 518-519.
[14] Enrique Ubieta, "Los héroes y la historia total", *Cubadebate*, October 25, 2010.

socialism's ideological legitimacy, based on official history, is experiencing its greatest breakdown.

The paradox brings us back to the relationship between legitimacy and history noted at the beginning of this essay. As a non-democratic régime's legitimizing discourse, the official history serves, among other purposes, to retain in the population's memory the civil war, the *stasis*, in other words, the fracturing of the community caused by the revolutionary order. This is why this discourse so often classifies subjects from the past into friends and enemies, heroes and traitors, patriots and anti-patriots, and expresses the genealogical link between these and the supporters or opponents of the régime in the present. Once opponents forsake the *stasis* and peacefully challenge a totalitarian legitimacy with a democratic one, the official history begins to lose adherents, and, what is worse, begins losing the support of the academic historiography that served as its sounding board.

Since the lack of democracy in Cuba will continue for some time, we should not rule out that the weakening of the official history could become a part of the normalizing tactics of the totalitarianism that wields the power. At international academic forums, for instance, official voices are already claiming that Cuba has no official history; rather, it has an ensemble of Marxist interpretations of the past. This is questionable in at least three ways: the official history *does* exist, as evidenced by the Council of State's historical publications; the history is not Marxist, but rather crudely nationalist; and some of the serious Marxists still remaining on the island do not subscribe to the hegemonic account of the official history.

The phenomenon of the decline of Cuba's official history should be analyzed as part of the recomposition of intellectual circles that is currently occurring inside and outside the island. It is difficult to even suggest that this recomposition will directly affect the generating of a political change or transition to democracy. That sort of phenomena seems to be more characteristic of the prolonged end of a régime than of the emergence of a new one. We can, however, confirm that the rewriting of Cuban history is already underway even if its principal emendations remain inaccessible to the majority of the island's citizens. Only when that rewriting of history is able to build an audience within the island will the dissemination of recollections become tangible and favor Cuban democratization.

THE EXECUTION OF REPUTATIONS: REPUBLICAN POLITICS. CARLOS MÁRQUEZ STERLING AND THE 1958 ELECTIONS

Uva de Aragón

There is an unforgivable vacuum in objective studies of Cuban history during the first half of the 20th century. Before the triumph of the Revolution in 1959, many textbooks ended on May 20, 1902. It seemed natural at the time, since there was a greater urgency to build the country's foundational myth. Furthermore, history was taking shape; many of its leading players were still alive and were even public figures. The chronological distance from this era was insufficient to enable a rigorous analysis of it with the proper perspective.

On January 1, 1959, Cuba experienced a tremendous split at all levels, and the manner of recording history was no exception. The vision of those who thenceforth wrote in exile—I mean people such as Leví Marrero, Calixto Masó, and Carlos Márquez Sterling, to name a few—was quite different from the narratives generated within the island, where, in the heat of the new ideological definitions and for many years afterwards, the period between 1902 and 1959 was demonized. Even today it is known as the mediatized Republic or the neo-Colony, the argument being that Cuba was completely under the thumb of the United States. Enough time has now elapsed to be able to study this chapter in greater detail and with less overshadowing passion, and this has begun to occur on both shores of the Florida Straits.

Let's review a few irrefutable facts. After years of struggle, during which the reformist initiatives of a Creole sector faltered under the intransigence of 19th-century Spain, the Mother Country pledged "up to the last *peseta* and the last soldier" in the war so as not to lose "the ever-loyal island of Cuba". The island was laid to waste. Even worse, Spain did not hand over the government of its former colony to the *mambís*[15], but to the U.S. military, which had joined the armed struggle at the last minute. The Cubans were therefore not present when peace was signed in Paris on December 10, 1898, and according to the agreement between both

---

[15] *Mambí* is a word used to describe a soldier who fought for Cuba's independence against the Spaniards. The *mambí* troops were composed of Cubans of all classes, from slaves to major landowners.

powers, many of the sources of wealth remained in Spanish or American hands, so that although Cubans were now independent, they were inheriting a country that did not actually belong to them. Let's also consider the effects of the single-crop system, the rise and fall in the price of sugar, the obstacles presented by outdated legal codes, the entrenched evils of corruption and political violence, and the constant interference in Cuban affairs by its northern neighbor. The Cubans were facing serious problems.

Despite these difficult circumstances, patriotism always ran high, there was an intellectual sector that gave itself over to the noble task of creating genuine citizens, and there were always very decent, honorable public voices and attitudes. Little by little, Cubans were able to lay the foundation for a new Republic, and, with great difficulty, the country began moving forward.

A key event was the Constituent Assembly of 1940, not just because the Cubans involved also provided themselves with a progressive constitution that included the aspirations for social justice that had driven the 1933 Revolution against the dictator Gerardo Machado, but because the various political parties, under no foreign influence, had pulled off an impeccable process of commitment and consensus. The new Constitution was a milestone and signaled the start of a period that was not without problems, but included an increasingly influential civil society and free elections in 1940, 1944 and 1948. This is why when Fulgencio Batista staged his coup d'état on March 10, 1952, a few months before the general elections, a profound malaise settled over Cuba. Batista's opposition took two main paths: the revolutionary and the political. Both proclaimed their objective to be the restoration of the 1940 Constitution, a symbol that meant a great deal to the citizens.

From that moment on, the view of history has differed in its interpretations, though they have nonetheless begun to coincide.

Fidel Castro, who turned out to be the main opposition figure to Batista by means of violence, had, during his years as a student at the University of Havana, acted as a leader of dubious reputation who was never able to win any student election nor place himself by democratic means at the head of his faculty or that of the university. He then became an active member of the Cuban Orthodox Party. His political aspirations were thwarted by Fulgencio Batista's coup, who in turn gave Castro the opportunity he was seeking for self-promotion via non-democratic means. He resorted to violence with the assault on the Moncada Barracks on July 26, 1953.

In Castro's celebrated address, *La historia me absolverá* (History Will Absolve Me), given before the magistrates on October 16, 1953 during his trial for leading the attack on the Moncada Barracks in July of that year, he said:

> *Who has told you that we have instigated an uprising against the Constitutional Powers of the State? Two things are patently clear. In the first place, the dictatorship oppressing the nation is not a constitutional but an unconstitutional power; it was engendered against the Constitution, above the Constitution, in violation of the legitimate Constitution of the Republic.*[16]

In this speech, he makes multiple references to the 1940 Constitution. At another point, he refers to the possible destruction of the documents containing the revolutionary laws, adding: "They are preserved in my memory. The first revolutionary law returned sovereignty to the people and proclaimed the 1940 Constitution to be the true supreme law of the State."

---

[16] Fidel Castro, *La historia me absolverá*, Buenos Aires, Ediciones del Pensamiento Nacional, 1993, p. 85.

In another passage, in order to show how Fulgencio Batista's coup of March 10, 1952 violated the Constitution, he mentions the punishments imposed by the Social Defense Code for various crimes, quoting: "He who would attempt to prevent or hinder the holding of general elections; [...] will incur the sanction of being deprived of his freedom for four-to-eight years."[17]

Castro was granted amnesty in May of 1955. After his release, he began recruiting supporters within the Orthodox Party to launch an armed struggle. In July of that year, he left for Mexico, where he organized the Granma's expedition in November, 1956.

From its initial mention in the *History Will Absolve Me* speech to the triumph of the Revolution on January 1, 1959, the restitution of the 1940 Constitution was one of Castro's chief promises to the Cuban people. However, as early as the Sierra Madre he had begun to violate the spirit of that fundamental law.

The first contradiction of constitutional principles became evident with the so-called Law One of the Sierra Madre, reestablishing the death penalty. Some months later he would again repudiate constitutional

---

[17] Ibid, p. 90.

principles with Law 2 of the Sierra, stipulating that death by "summary execution" would be the punishment meted out to those who stood for the elections that had been called for November 3, 1958. These laws were not written to gather dust on a forgotten shelf. On the guerrilla battlegrounds, numerous executions by firing squad took place not just of soldiers charged with war crimes, but of members of the rebel army who were executed for some breach of discipline following improvised trials with scant procedural guarantees. Furthermore, at the time of the 1958 elections, all of the candidates—even, or perhaps in particular, those of the opposition—were constantly being threatened, intimidated and were targets of assassination attempts, in some cases successful ones. "Nicolás Rivero Agüero, candidate for councilman representing Santiago de Cuba and brother of the government coalition's presidential candidate, was shot dead through the back."[18] Also assassinated were the trade unionist Felipe Navea, the cattle breeder Rosendo Collazo, and Aníbal Vega, brother of Víctor Vega, provincial president of the opposition Free Party (*Partido Libre*). The latter case was particularly scandalous because his house in Camagüey was broken into and bullets flew through the bars of his young daughter's crib, whom he had just put down for a nap. Miraculously, the girl

---

[18] Jorge García Montes and Antonio Alonso Ávila. *Historia del Partido Comunista de Cuba*. Miami, Ediciones Universal, 1970, p. 572.

was unhurt.[19] In a radio speech to the Cuban people on Radio Rebelde on October 24, 1958, Fidel Castro himself revealed his complete rejection of electoral methods: "Elections in the middle of a war? Whatever the result of these elections, whatever name the dictatorship decides to write on the ballots, the Revolution will continue inexorably on its course."[20] Contemporary documents illustrate both the constant radio rants telling people to stay home on November 3, 1958 and not vote, as well as the violent acts in which the most senior revolutionary leaders, such as Che Guevara, participated.[21]

Fidel Castro continually promised to restore the constitutional guarantees violated by Batista, all the while enacting his own lethal revolutionary laws which he arbitrarily applied. He violently sabotaged all forms of political dialogue or negotiation that could have put an end to the Batista régime, so as to be able

---

[19] Ibid. See also Carlos Márquez Sterling. *Historia de Cuba. Desde Colón hasta Castro.* New York, Las Américas Publishing Company, 1963, p. 423.

[20] Andrés Castillo Bernal. *Cuando esta guerra se acabe. De las montañas al llano.* Fidel Castro's manifesto to the Cuban people on the first eighty days of the campaign in the Sierra Maestra, February 20, 1957. Havana, Editorial de Ciencias Cubanas, 2000, p. 267.

[21] Ibid, p. 267-279.

to justify the need for his revolutionary movement and avoid finding himself forced to lay down arms and renounce seizing power.[22]

Through these methods of intimidation, he was effectively successful in convincing a number of politicians of the day who opposed Batista to decide to give up looking for civic solutions and approve, tacitly or explicitly, of the insurrectional violence. Such was not the case of Carlos Márquez Sterling, a lawyer, university professor, twelve-year congressman and president of the House of Representatives, who in 1940 had acted brilliantly as chairman of the Constituent Assembly. In addition, Márquez Sterling was validated by the track record of his father, don Manuel, a journalist and diplomat of acknowledged patriotism who had negotiated and signed the abolition of the Platt Amendment,[23] as

---

[22] Ibid. For examples, see *"No al pacto de Miami"*, pp. 476-477, and Jorge Ibarra Guitart, *Sociedad de Amigos de la República (SAR), Historia de una mediación 1952-1958*. Havana, Editorial de Ciencias Sociales, 2003, pp. 98-99. The author quotes statements by Fidel Castro in 1956 given in response to the SAR's mediation to try to find a peaceful solution to the Cuban problem in which he professes being in favor of immediate general elections, and others from 1978 in which he asserts that ever since his release, his strategy has been one of fighting to "show there was no political solution".

[23] This amendment was imposed by the United States on the Cubans during the country's occupation, and together with the Constitution of 1901, it allowed, among other things, intervention

well as by Márquez Sterling's own reputation as an honest politician in a milieu within which there was unquestionable corruption coexisting with civil servants of proven honesty. It was the latter's unjust lot to bear the brunt of the negative view of political circles, which had been implanted by those aspiring to replace the incumbent leaders or opposition members who had been elected to public office. Political aspirations are legitimate so long as they are inspired by the desire to serve, not by the desire to make one's fortune, as regrettably was sometimes the case. At the same time, certain media outlets for which sensationalism was a way of increasing their circulation and influence also contributed to creating a negative view of politics among a majority of the Cuban population.[24]

---

by Cuba's northern neighbor in its affairs in order to protect lives and economic interests. For a history of the negotiations that led to the amendment's repeal in 1934, see Manuel Márquez Sterling, *Las conferencias del Shoreham*, Mexico, Ediciones Botas, 1933.

[24] The most notable case of false public defamation involved Eduardo Chibás, a prominent figure within the Orthodox Party who in his radio programs promoted sweeping away corruption. He pointed an accusatory finger at the genuine administrations of Ramón Grau San Martín and Carlos Prío Socarrás, and became a true idol of the Cuban people. However, Aureliano Sánchez Arango, minister of education under Prío, accused him of being a "master of defamation" and "a false apostle of lies, of demagoguery and of slander". Chibás had accused Aureliano of "stealing funds from public schools to buy an *hacienda* in Guatemala". Chibás

(I should pause here to clarify that I have very close links to Carlos Márquez Sterling because he married my mother in 1956, three years after the death of my father, the physician and university professor Ernesto R. de Aragón. These family ties, however, offer certain advantages. In order to avoid any possible subjectivity, I have taken inordinate care to document everything I have written about this topic here and elsewhere. I also have the advantage of having witnessed some of the narrated events and of having had access to first-hand documental sources.)

Carlos Márquez Sterling was the main opposition presidential candidate running against the ruling party's candidate Andrés Rivero Agüero. One of Márquez's campaign slogans was "Neither with boots nor with bullets; with votes". He offered the revolu-

---

promised evidence he did not have, and unable to provide it, shot himself on August 15, 1951 during one of his radio programs, not realizing he was no longer on the air. He died a few days later on August 26. Castro tried to use Chibás's funeral as an excuse to march on Government Palace and overthrow Prío, but he found no support. Certainly the death of the passionate orthodox leader, who did not sympathize with Castro, ended up benefiting him. Although no evidence was ever found of corruption on the part of Aureliano Sánchez Arango, and despite books written by historians and descendants, there are still references to Sánchez Arango that question his honesty. Among others, see Georgie Anne Geyer, *El patriarca de las guerrillas. La historia oculta de Fidel Castro*, San José, Costa Rica, 1991, pp. 73-82.

tionaries a general amnesty, guarantees so they would lay down arms and organize themselves politically, and, should he win the vote, to call a general election in two years instead of the four the Constitution stipulated his mandate should last, an election in which he would not run. He sought to pave the way for a transitional government.[25] He received many "messages" from the revolutionaries and from Castro personally during his political campaign. I will share just two of them. The first was an attempt to stab him, on February 2, 1955, when members of the 26th of July Movement burst into the halls of the Artística Gallega during the general meeting of the Party of the Free People (*Partido del Pueblo Libre*) during which he declared his candidacy for the elections.[26] The other example is the message that was sent by Castro to Márquez Sterling telling him to withdraw his candidacy for the elections, to support the Revolution, and he would appoint him president upon his victory. Márquez Sterling replied that that was not how he wanted to reach the presiden-

---

[25] See the front-page article by Márquez Sterling in *Diario La Marina*, Havana, August 9, 1958.

[26] Carlos Márquez Sterling, *Historia de Cuba. Desde Colón hasta Castro*, New York, Las Américas Publishing Company, 1963, pp. 416-417.

cy, and that Castro should recommend citizens to vote instead of threatening them.[27]

The argument that was put forth against the elections was that they "played Batista's game", in other words, that they would help legitimize the dictatorship. Márquez Sterling, in contrast, declared that no fraud would take place if there was a vote *en masse*; and should there be fraud under such circumstances, it would confirm the régime's lack of good faith, whereupon "ten Sierras Madres" would spring up. His belief that Batista would respect the electoral outcome was not unfounded. It was based, above all, on conversations with then prime minister Jorge García Montes during which the high-ranking official promised, on behalf of Batista, to respect the electoral results, while in return Márquez Sterling gave his word that the Free People's Party would not conspire against the government. There was also the precedent that Batista had held honest elections in 1944 and transferred the presidency to the Authentic Party's Ramón Grau San Martín. Furthermore, logic dictated that Batista would understand the impossibility of remaining in power by force, and that accepting his party's electoral defeat offered the country a solution without any need for bloodshed.

---

[27] Ibid, p. 434.

However, as Márquez Sterling had predicted, voter participation decreased due to the violent harassment that was taking place, thus paving the way for electoral fraud and for the civil war's increased importance after the electoral fiasco.

Márquez Sterling was arrested on January 4, 1959, and although he was allowed to return home the following day, he remained under house arrest until March of that year. His bank accounts and law firm were seized. At the same time, a rumor began to spread that false evidence was being gathered against him in order to prosecute him and remove him from his university post. In early June, the newspaper *Combate* published a reproduction of three checks issued by Batista's government for $50,000, each payable to CMS. No signature appeared on the back indicating the checks had been cashed and by whom. The newspaper nevertheless claimed they represented payments to Márquez Sterling for participating in the elections. One month later, on July 13, 1959, Márquez Sterling sought refuge in the Venezuelan Embassy and left the country. He died in Miami at age 92 in 1991.

For fifty years, these checks that have not been shown to having been cashed and that do not bear Márquez Sterling's name, as is mandatory, but rather his initials, have been the only purported evidence the régime has presented of the bribe he is alleged to have received for participating in the electoral farce. Nonetheless, this information appears in Cuba's National Archives and in books as recent as one published in 2008 in which the amount has risen to $250,000, but with no proof whatsoever as to who was the true beneficiary of the famous checks, nor of their having been cashed by anyone.[28] Not only has no documentary proof or trace of any monetary transaction between Batista's government and Márquez Sterling ever been produced, but once in exile he lived on what he earned from his work until his retirement at age 80, and died poor.

In *Batista. Últimos días en el poder* [Batista. Final Days in Power] by José Luis Padrón and Luis Adrián Betancourt, the authors recount how in the home of the engineer Salazar, Batista "had a clandestine electoral office set up (...) where he printed identical duplicates of the electoral ballots" meant to replace the legitimate ones "once the voting had concluded on election

---

[28] Guillermo Jiménez, *Los propietarios de Cuba 1958*. Havana, Instituto del Libro Cubano, Tercera Edición, 2008, p. 503. Márquez Sterling does not appear as a property owner because by 1956 he had sold his only property, a house in the Víbora district, and had moved into the house of his second wife, Uva Hernández-Cata, Aragón's widow. The reference appears in an entry about his daughter-in-law's father Antonio Sánchez Vaillant, the owner of a car dealership.

day".[29] The obvious question is: If the opposition candidate had been "bought" by the government, what necessity would there have been to prepare duplicate ballots and switch the original ones in the electoral colleges?

Márquez Sterling is by no means the only Cuban politician whose reputation the Revolution has tried to ruin. He is just one example among many whom I chose because of my detailed prior knowledge. The issue is not merely that of destroying the reputation of individuals, but of an entire 56-year chapter in the country's history, barely longer than the revolutionary era's 51 years, and of not acknowledging the struggles for social justice nor the defense of national interests in the face of the voraciousness of spurious interests and U.S. interference by so many honoured politicians and intellectuals of the day, unless they belonged to the Communist Party or supported Fidel Castro.

The U.S. historian Theodore Draper records the conflict faced by Castro and his followers between the

---

[29] José Luis Padrón and Luis Adrián Betancourt. *Batista. Últimos días en el poder*. Havana, Ediciones Unión, 2008, p. 16. This information accurately coincides with that which appears in Gabriel E. Taborda, *Palabras Esperadas. Memorias de Francisco H. Tabernilla Palmero*, Miami, Ediciones Universales, 2009. Tabernilla was a general staff officer in the Cuban Army and personal aide to Fulgencio Batista.

promises Castro made in order to come to power and his true intentions. Draper underscores that "some of Castro's supporters began reediting history—a mere two years after the end of the struggle!—through a selection process that eluded any mention of such promises".[30] In reality, throughout 1959, Fidel Castro had already begun ranting and raving against everything "from before" in his numerous speeches, including the old constitutional laws, and instead imposed those he called "revolutionary".

Although in recent years some intellectuals in Cuba have apparently become interested in reviewing the first half of the 20th century, these efforts are often insufficient. For instance, there seems to be a push toward once again pointing out the value of the 1940 Constitution. A few months ago Fidel Castro himself acknowledged that "Before the beginning of the Cold War, Cuba itself had a fairly progressive constitution, there was hope and there existed possibilities of democratic changes although never, of course, that of a social revolution."[31]

---

[30] Theodore Draper, *La revolución de Castro. Mitos y realidades.* Mexico, Libros Mex, 1962, p. 21.

[31] *Granma*, Havana, April 9, 2010.

In a recent commemoration that took place in Havana of the 70th anniversary of the signing of the vilified 1940 Constitution, the speakers praised its merits. Armando Hart Dávalos described the document "as one of the most progressive of its time".[32] He also said:

> It expresses Cuban political thought in the forties, achieved through public consensus and formalized by the Constituent Assembly, in the presence of figures from both the right as well as a distinguished representation of communists and revolutionary forces from the fight against Machado.
>
> Notable representatives of bourgeois conservative thinking were Emilio Núñez Portuondo, Carlos Márquez Sterling, José Manuel Cortina, and Alfredo Hornedo, among others, and on the side of the progressive and revolutionary forces one would have to mention Blas Roca, Eduardo Chibás, Salvador García Agüero, and Juan Marinello.

Hart, however, makes no mention whatsoever of the democratic skill with which Márquez Sterling, the purported bourgeois conservative, presided over the Assembly, much less acknowledges that the number of assemblymen who were Communist Party members was a mere six out of a total of 76, so the constitution's

---

[32] Armando Hart Dávalos, "Constitución de 1940: un hito esencial de la tradición jurídica cubana", *Juventud Rebelde*, October 10, 2010.

progressive nature would have been impossible without the backing of many of its members. In reality, most of the literature on the Constituent Assembly published in Cuba makes no mention of Márquez Sterling, nor do the history books do him justice. Even quite a few of those written in other countries do not even mention the 1958 elections and overlook the possibility Cuba had at the time of finding prosperity and social justice via a different path. This alternative narrative, suppressed until now, would underscore that history is never linear and that Cuba's specific path as of 1959 was not responding to an alleged historical *necessity*, nor was it *inevitable*. However, in order to sustain an official historiographic perspective that presented the régime that emerged after 1959 as the only *feasible* society on the island given its prior history, it became necessary to silence, erase, and discredit prominent figures, and distort important events in republican history.

Changes lie ahead in Cuba's near future, and they cannot be limited to economic, political, and social ones. As Cambridge University has acknowledged[33], the post-conflict phase presents a colossal challenge: the salvaging of identities and historical recollections.

---

[33] Cambridge University is promoting a program on "Identity and Conflict: Cultural Heritage and the Re-construction of Identities after Conflict". See http://www.cric.arch.cam.ac.uk

The shooting-down of the reputation of the republican era's political class in Cuba should be revisited by historians who are able to look at the past with fresh eyes. The objective study of the society we inherited from the *mambí* struggles—crammed then as now with its defects, failures, rascals, corruption, but not entirely without merit, noble initiatives, and upstanding human beings—is an indispensable task in building a better future for Cuba. This is not a matter of personal opinion. In Liu Xiaobo's celebrated Charter 08, the Chinese dissident and brand-new recipient of the Nobel Peace Prize proposes under No. 19: "TRUTH IN RECONCILIATION. We should restore the reputations of all people, including their family members, who suffered political stigma in the political campaigns of the past or who have been labeled as criminals because of their thought, speech, or faith".[34] This formula will be just as useful for a reconciliation process in Cuba.

---

[34] See p.3 of Yu Zhang's foreword entry in Part III of Charter 08, "What We Advocate", under the online publications subheading of **http://www.liuxiaobo.eu**, in the *Who is Liu XiaoBo?* menu section.

Carlos Márquez Sterling with Nestor Carbonell
during the 1958 political campaign

Carlos Márquez Sterling with his wife Uva Hernández Catá leaving
his house in Havana on his way to vote, November 3, 1958

Publicity for the Party of the Free People (Partido del Pueblo Libre) and its candidate, Carlos Márquez Sterling, during the electoral process of 1958. The original photo caption reads: "Who is conspiring against the happiness of Cubans? Those who tell you beforehand they'll be sandbagging you, or those who call on the people to avoid that sandbagging?..." "Don't accept the sandbagging in advance; force the Government to sandbag you if it dares to do it again. How can you force it? Well, by having your registration card and going out to vote..." Carlos Márquez Sterling

Carlos Márquez Sterling in exile, New York, 1975

THE CHARACTER ASSASSINATION OF CUBAN BUSINESSMEN. AN ANALYSIS OF THE SMEAR CAMPAIGNS AGAINST AMADEO BARLETTA

Juan Antonio Blanco

I. The Origins and Goal of This Research

The following exposé is a summary of a lengthy and as yet unpublished investigation. First, however, it seems important to give a brief commentary, by way of personal introduction, on the reasons that motivated it.

I have a doctorate in History of International Relations, and throughout my life my duties have been split between those of a professor and an academic researcher in the aforementioned field, and those of a diplomat and a political analyst. For ten years (1987-1997) and almost since its inception, I belonged to the National Commission in Cuba, which awards scientific degrees in History. As a Commission member, I and other colleagues were responsible for evaluating doctoral theses in History; this academic activity compelled me to conduct the critical analysis of the works submitted not only in regards to their conclusions, but also to the methodological rigor used by the doctoral candidates.

Following the events of June 28, 2009 that ousted Honduran president Manuel Zelaya, I began preparing an article comparing Franklin D. Roosevelt's "good neighbor" policy with the one that President Barack Obama seemingly intended to try out during the Honduran crisis. Thus, I found that if Honduras was the first test of the new hemispheric policy announced by President Obama at the Summit of the Americas, held in Trinidad and Tobago in April of that year, then for Franklin D. Roosevelt the test had been the conflict with Mussolini concerning the imprisonment of the Italian consul in the Dominican Republic, as ordered by the dictator Leónidas Trujillo in 1935.[35] Curiously, the diplomat at the center of such an important hemispheric and international occurrence, Amadeo Barletta Barletta, was a prosperous Italian immigrant who

---

[35] As is common knowledge, President Franklin D. Roosevelt tried distancing himself from his predecessor's "Big Stick" policy by announcing a new hemispheric relationship, which he called that of the "Good Neighbor". In 1935 an event in the Dominican Republic tested Washington's ability to protect its interests without having to interfere or intervene in the affairs of other countries in the region.

would subsequently play a prominent role in Cuba's economic history.

The dictator Rafael Leónidas Trujillo said he had discovered a conspiracy was in the works to assassinate him, and among those arrested was Italy's honorary consul at the time, Amadeo Barletta. Because of Trujillo's smooth relationship with the United States, he thought that arresting the Italian consul was a transgression Washington would forgive, especially if he was able to provide a confession that would serve as of some sort or evidence of the diplomat's guilt. Trujillo's suspicion was not totally unfounded, since Amadeo had, indeed, offered financial aid to General Desiderio Arias's[36] group on a previous occasion, which was planning to overthrow Trujillo, although the dictator was unaware of this fact. In reality, Trujillo did not like Barletta and placed no trust in him.[37]

---

[36] Bernardo Vega, *Desiderio Arias y Trujillo se escriben*, Dominican Republic, Fundación Cultural Dominicana, 2009, pp. 150-151, 153, 178, 243, 248-249, 281, 289.

[37] According to FBI file 100-15049 put together by S. F. Ducibella on November 21, 1941, Barletta admitted to his friends at General Motors that he had accepted the post of Italian Consul in the Dominican Republic—which did not add any significant benefit to his already prosperous businesses—in the hope that it would provide him with some measure of immunity from Trujillo. After the Italian government played all its cards to extract him from the Dominican leader's dungeons and asked him to accept the post of

When Barletta was held in 1935 at the sinister Nigua[38] prison, Trujillo's principal motivation for his capture was the confiscation of his properties, in par-

---

honorary consul in Havana, Barletta once again accepted, although in this case in gratitude for his rescue. (S. F. Ducibella, *Amadeo Barletta. File No. 100-15049*, New York, Federal Bureau of Investigation, November 21, 1941. National Archives and Records Administration (NARA), Maryland.)

[38] According to the accounts of those who experienced the nightmare of being imprisoned in Nigua prison, it was the worst possible fate. (*Nigua* is a type of sand flea that embeds itself in the flesh, especially the feet, and can prevent a person from walking.) At the time, the saying was "it is better to have a hundred *niguas* in your foot than to set one foot inside Nigua". Raúl Roa, in the Introduction to *Una Gestapo en América* (A Gestapo in the Americas), describes it as follows:

No imagination, no matter how fertile or diabolical, is capable of inventing the atrocities at Nigua prison and at the fortress of Homenaje. It would only be possible to compare them to those perpetrated by the Nazis in the concentration camps. Rarely has human dignity suffered such brutal abuses as in these crime-filled dens, places just a few hours' flight from the Cuban coast. No commiseration for the weak, nor mercy for the sick, nor consideration for affliction. Everyone, old and young, black and white, rich and poor, intellectuals and laymen, shackled to the shared torment of forced labor, the disgusting scraps, the maddening solitude of "solitary", the merciless abandonment, the ravages of malaria, the machete, the windlass and the "cantaclaro" [a multi-tailed whipping device made from wires]. *Everyone, absolutely everyone, offended and humiliated, day after day, hour after hour, minute after minute, by a sinister horde of criminals [...]* (Raúl Roa, Introduction to *Una Gestapo en América*, by Juan Isidro Jimenes Grullón, Santo Domingo, Sociedad Dominicana de Bibliófilos, 2003, pp. 15-23).

ticular that of a tobacco enterprise that competed with another company owned by the dictator in the same industry. For a while, the State Department in Washington resisted the pressure brought to bear by the powerful General Motors company (a partner of Santo Domingo Motors, owned by Amadeo Barletta in the Dominican Republic) and by Philadelphia's Penn Tobacco Company (a partner of the Dominican Tobacco Company, also owned by Barletta) for approaching Trujillo in support of Barletta. Things changed, however, when an Italian diplomat finally was able to see Barletta in his cell and reported to his government and to the State Department that the prisoner's evident physical and mental deterioration was a result of the brutal interrogations he was being subjected to in order to extract a self-incriminating confession about having planned the alleged assassination.

Rome then decided to test the limits between the recently launched Good Neighbor policy and the persistence of the Monroe Doctrine mentality: If the U.S. had truly renounced the Monroe Doctrine, and therefore would not think it necessary to intervene in this matter, Il Duce could carry out a show of naval force with his own warships in the Dominican Republic in order to persuade that country's government that it must unconditionally release the Italian consul.[39] The reality is that from that moment on, Washington sped up its efforts, and managed to persuade Trujillo to free Barletta.

After weeks of solitary confinement, violent interrogations, having revolvers pointed at him and witnessing other prisoners return, shattered, to their cells, following torture sessions, and then witnessing them being finished off, Barletta was finally released and the decrees and legal sanctions whereby his properties had been confiscated and diplomatic privileges revoked were overturned. To his bemusement, he was summoned to have a personal interview with Trujillo, who, with his habitual cynicism, blamed his subalterns for

---

[39] Two telegrams from Mr. Schoenfeld, ambassador to the Dominican Republic, to the U.S. Secretary of State confirm that the Italian ambassador threatened to send warships to Santo Domingo if the United States did not resolve the Barletta situation. In the second message, Schoenfeld wrote: "He again indicated that his government might decide to make a naval demonstration here and sounded me as to our attitude in such eventuality." Schoenfeld, *File 339.115 General Motors Co./95: Telegram,* Santo Domingo, May 10, 1935. Shoenfeld, *File 339.115 General Motors Co./85: Telegram,* Santo Domingo, May 8, 1935. National Archives and Records Administration (NARA), Maryland.

Some historians doubted this conversation had actually taken place, but these official U.S. documents I found confirm it.

all that had occurred and made a point of dismissing the minister of Foreign Relations.[40]

While analyzing the 1935 incident, I came across an unusual amount of information on Amadeo Barletta, recently posted on various websites, almost all of which had been based on the arguments provided by a single Cuban writer. I therefore decided to conduct independent research on the reasons for this phenomenon and on the validity of the serious accusations made against Barletta.

The name Amadeo Barletta was an almost forgotten memory from my childhood, blurred by the passage of time. His life and mine had never crossed paths, except for the fact that we both lived on the same island. I was eleven years old when he went into exile, and the universe mapped out different and opposite routes for us, but the accusations made against him in the abovementioned more recent references seemed to be intertwined with a more far-reaching ob-

---

[40] J. F. McGurk, *Memorandum: Conversation between Amadeo Barletta, Dominican Tobacco Company and Dominican Motors Company, Mr. Clark, Puerto Rico Representative of General Motors Corporation and Mr. McGurk, assistant to Secretary Welles, File 339.115 General Motors Export Co./198*, Washington, Department of State, June 5, 1935. National Archives and Records Administration (NARA), Maryland.

jective: the damning of an entire social class and of the republican era that preceded the 1959 revolution.

The central argument, repeated with the tedious insistence of all typical propaganda, was not just that Amadeo Barletta was a gangster, but that the Republic of Cuba, from the 1930s until the 1959 revolution, was a criminal state controlled by the Italian-American mafia, which was in cahoots with the intelligence services of the United States and local politicians such as Fulgencio Batista. According to this criterion, the economic prosperity achieved by the island prior to 1959 was a result of the murky business dealings of the partnership between these forces.

At first glance, it seems like a novel variation on the traditional focus of official revolutionary historiography, which invariably presents Cuba as a wretched and corrupt island, entirely under U.S. control—and thus lacking in any indigenous political or economic development—that is finally rescued from this ignominious situation by Fidel Castro. The new ingredient in this scenario was the mafia as a principal player in Cuban history. The question this immediately raised in my mind was why and under what circumstances had the government sponsors of that official history felt the need to give their usual lines of attack this new twist. To dismiss it as pedestrian was not a valid assessment.

Western pop culture, produced primarily in the United States and exported all over the planet, reveals an ongoing fascination with gangsters and the topic of the mafia. Fiction becomes reality once it appears on the pages of best-sellers and jumps to the screen in Hollywood. Academicians, historians in particular, cannot justify their scholarly pursuits and ignore such trends. Those responsible for producing ideological propaganda are very well aware of the advantages to be found in getting Hollywood to accept their premises and include them in their film scripts.[41]

Although it was impossible for me to get involved in research of great depth on that particular issue, I thought it would be productive to unravel one of the more novel strings of yarn from that skein: the alleged criminal history of the businessman Amadeo Barletta, about which no history book—not even an official one—had until then anything to say.

In addressing this topic, I preferred not to formulate any hypotheses in advance, and instead chose to

---

[41] While aiming to characterize the 125,000 Cubans who left via the port of El Mariel for the United States in 1980 as "scum", the Cuban government released convicts from prison and included them in that exodus. The image of the "Marielito" as a criminal, however, was constructed by the film *Scarface*. The character of the exiled criminal Tony Montana, magnificently portrayed by Al Pacino, has been cemented in society's imagination ever since.

develop a three-pronged strategy that entailed the following:

a) attempting to reconstruct chronologically, and as precisely as possible, the life of Amadeo Barletta, and position it within the historical context in which he lived;

b) refraining from formulating any advanced hypotheses, and instead first trying to corroborate those already in circulation by going straight to the sources, then comparing those assertions with new evidence and conducting a critical analysis of the methodological rigor shown by those authors; and

c) dismissing assertions based on presumptions or suspicions— those along the lines of conspiracy theories— as well as those not based on conclusive, authentic evidence (testaments, documents), the veracity of which can be confirmed.

The idea was to establish a factual overview of Amadeo Barletta's biography, to see how it interconnected with the times in which he lived, and to be able to confirm or reject whatever was true or false regarding the accusations leveled against him. If in trying to corroborate these accusations it became obvious they were false or not well-founded, I would then have to provide a plausible explanation as to why a growing number of authors and websites consistently repeated them either directly or indirectly.

In other words, I felt compelled to investigate and explain not just this important figure's true history, but also to analyze the reasons and forces behind the recent and growing accusations regarding this individual, should they not be substantiated during the course of my investigation. This objective thus entailed that I embark on the critical analysis of the sources used by the authors to back up their allegations. It likewise became necessary—beyond their greater or lesser methodological rigor—to decipher the motivations and context that could have led the authors to articulate their arguments in this way. Finally, but no less important, I was obliged to inquire into the forces behind the growing speed garnered by the dissemination of those reports over the last few years.

This investigation involved a considerable investment of time, of which I was then short, but the subject was fascinating and promised to shed light on other parallel processes of the history of the era I was investigating, the understanding of which was important to me in order to analyze current processes. This is why I decided, upon finishing my article on the Honduran crisis, to devote six months to producing preliminary research on the life of Amadeo Barletta and the accusations against him.

Changes are coming to Cuba, and reconstructing the past as precisely and non-ideologically as possible becomes necessary in a society whose official institutions have been distorting it for half a century. It is not a matter of replacing one official history with another, but of constructing a plural interpretation of our past that makes use of the various narratives available, without allowing for the deliberate construction of falsehoods that are presented as unanimous truths.

Historiography is always pluralist; propaganda is not. Historians of any ideological bent pursue truth in accordance to the hard facts. Propaganda is interested not in truth, but in effectively manipulating perceptions in the service of a result that has already been decided.

II.   Ideology, Propaganda and Historiography

Character assassination is the deliberate destruction of the reputation of a person, social group, institution, or period through the combined use of various propaganda techniques and covert acts of disinformation. Those encouraging this activity may or may not use real life-based information, but they present the facts out of context and distort their meaning in order to make completely false accusations believable. The aim of character assassination is to cause the victim to be rejected by their community, family, colleagues and/or the general public. Oftentimes, it is a strategy that can precede or proceed in tandem with an additional form of assassination, either physical or financial.

The historiographer faces the multi-faceted and complex task of analyzing the historical context within which these state-sponsored character assassination campaigns emerge, the motivations behind each of them, the manner in which they operate, and the people and institutions associated with them.

The various official assaults on the businessman Amadeo Barletta are a paradigmatic example of how state-sponsored campaigns designed for the character assassination of the Cuban government's adversaries are gestated. This is why I chose him as the example in my analysis of the official mechanism used for character assassination in Cuba.

This example, like many others, does not constitute as evidence of the submission of Cuban social scientists and their institutions to political power. On the contrary, over the last five decades, the usual pattern has been one of a perennial tug-of-war between the professional vocation for methodological rigor displayed by historians and the attempt to discipline their thinking and writing via the authorities' carrot-and-stick policy.

Very often, those in power have had to use officially-sanctioned writers with no professional training or recognition as historians or political analysts to replace the voices of the genuine social scientists who, as a rule, resist or elude the demand that they lend their pens to dubious hypotheses. The arbitrary way in which ideological control mechanisms have artificially inflated the intellectual backgrounds of writers who unconditionally offered their services to the powers-that-be while keeping other academicians—even genuine Marxists, who are critical precisely for that reason—on the editorial and teaching sidelines has always been a cause for resentment. Situations such as these are particularly annoying to those social scientists, historians in particular, who take seriously both their socialist calling as well as the methodological rigor upheld by the dignity of their profession. To them, when they are not bound by dogmatism (which, depending on the case, can be sincere or opportunist), Marxism is not a propaganda tool, but a school of theoretical thought open to change and innovation.

Historical studies have always been viewed in many societies as sources for the legitimization of power. In Cuba's case, in addition to trying to justify the historical "inevitability", and therefore legitimacy, of the revolutionary process, they have also been used as excuses to justify any scandal or endemic shortcoming as either an isolated incident or the lesser evil, considering the "horrible capitalist past" whence the current régime emerged.[42]

However, the task of historians and the various historiographic outputs they generate from their varying interpretive paradigms are one thing, while propaganda and character assassinations are quite another.

---

[42] The determinist and linear view of the process of history fostered since the 19th century by the most orthodox of Marxist viewpoints entered into permanent crisis with the events of 1989 and the crumbling of the régimes that had declared themselves as having a monopoly on the road to the future. Since then, it has been indisputable that more than one possible future always dwells in the present, until one of them — or a combination of all of them — prevails. The logical corollary to this assertion is that if there is always more than one possible future, then there also was always more than one possible past. The civil war against Batista was waged by forces from both democratic and totalitarian leanings. The conflicts between both sides later found manifestation in a new civil war beginning in 1959. The present currently being experienced in Cuba was not "inevitable" nor did it express a historical "necessity". It was merely one of the potential futures in 1958. The problems afflicting the island could also have been addressed via the social democratic alternative, which in Cuba was just as patriotic as its radical counterpart. But this complex and non-linear understanding of historical evolution is not the one disseminated by the current Cuban government via its cultural, educational, and propaganda machines.

Fact and Fiction (Historiography versus Conspiracy Theories)

In closed societies, political institutions bring pressure to bear on historical research in order to investigative results that back up the current policies of the régime in question and legitimize its past actions. Academicians who distance themselves from officially sanctioned axioms are viewed with suspicion, and expose themselves to sometimes open, or sometimes more subtle reprisals.

One challenge to this investigation is the insurmountable distance between fact and fiction when the rigor of historiographic methods has been rejected in favor of conclusions pre-decided by some officially constructed or approved conspiracy theory. It is very likely, for instance, that when demonstrating the arbitrariness of the alleged "evidence" put forward against Amadeo Barletta, it will be said that the lack of evidence pointing the finger at him does not prove his innocence because such evidence was probably hidden or destroyed. Under a totalitarian régime, it is the accused who must prove their innocence with evidence, while the public prosecutors demand that they be sentenced out of "belief".

The Dismantling of National Capitalism

The forces that gradually managed to centralize power between the revolutionary triumph in 1959 and the spring of 1961 condemned Cuban capitalism and its business class to death. However, they could not from the outset reveal their true intent, for fear that their future victims would join together early on in a united front. This is why the so-called Fundamental Law of 1959, which replaced the 1940 Constitution, in defense of which Batista fought, prohibited the confiscation of property except in cases where there were "reasonable indications of illegal gain" under the protection of the overthrown dictatorial régime.

This approach enabled an expropriation process that began with the most obvious cases of "guilt", and progressively spread to other individuals who, although innocent, were slandered in the media as pro-Batista so as to create a favorable environment for confiscating their assets. The Cuban bourgeoisie seems to have been slow to realize that the expropriations already had little to do with any evidence that may have been put forward by the public prosecutor against the accused. They did not realize that today the government would go after others, and tomorrow, after them.[43]

---

[43] An interesting case is that of the sugar magnate Julio Lobo.

The issue was not, as many believed, one of "excesses" committed by young, inexperienced but well-intentioned radicals. What was really occurring was the setting in motion of a master plan to eliminate not just the bourgeoisie, but the entire free market, which by 1968 would be completely government-controlled and in the hands of a single-party government. The expropriations would begin in 1959 with those from the previous régime found to be genuinely guilty of corruption, then moving on to the highest echelons of the bourgeoisie, and finally encompassing, in March 1968, all those who were self-employed or owned a micro-business. In the early 1960s, however, it was crucial for Fidel Castro and the nucleus of radical leaders in his immediate circle to deprive his enemies of the financial resources and means of communication (independent of the government) necessary for them to have a means of putting forward their view of the situation.

This strategy's implementation, initially carried out against large businesses, concluded in 1968 with the so-called "revolutionary offensive" against thou-

---

Aware of Lobo's exceptional industrial talent and financial expertise, Ernesto Guevara made him an offer he deemed generous: to expropriate him, but offer him a post as adviser to the revolutionary government. (John Paul Rathbone. *The Sugar King of Havana; The Rise and Fall of Julio Lobo, Cuba's Last Tycoon*, The Penguin Press HC, 2010).

sands of small and medium sized businesses, and with the nationwide termination of self-employment. Self-employed carpenters and plumbers would, in due course, also be accused of constituting a kind of counterrevolutionary force.

By March 13, 1968, Fidel Castro no longer had to disguise his objectives: "Clearly and categorically, we must say that we intend to eliminate every manifestation of private enterprise, clearly and categorically".[44] However, he continued to use the same technique against these modest entrepreneurs that had been previously used against the higher echelons of the business class, i.e., destroying their reputation: "If a lot of people are asking themselves what kind of revolution this is that nine years later still allows such a class of parasites, they are absolutely right in asking. And we believe we must firmly begin to set for ourselves the goal of putting an end to any parasitical activity remaining in the Revolution".[45]

This gradual process of eliminating all commercial relationships in Cuba and annihilating the social sectors associated with them was always the true *leitmotif* concealed behind each individual accusation. This is

---

[44] Fidel Castro. Speech during the Commemoration of the 11th Anniversary of the Action of March 13, 1957 held on the steps of the University of Havana, Castro Speech Data Base, LANIC, University of Texas at Austin, **http://lanic.utexas.edu/**.

[45] Ibid.

why those who were victims of unjust condemnation did not have any possibility of escaping their fate, no matter how much evidence they were able to gather regarding their innocence.

On this issue, the Cuban revolution imitated the Bolshevik spirit and methodology of dismissing an individual's guilt or innocence, and exclusively putting the "guilt" of a social class on trial. No one expressed the nature of this approach better than a deputy chief of Lenin's secret police (Cheka), the feared Latvian M. I. Latsis, when he explains the true meaning of "red terror":

> *The Extraordinary Commission is neither an investigating commission nor a tribunal. It is an organ of struggle, acting on the home front of a civil war. It does not judge the enemy: it strikes him (...) We are not carrying out war against individuals. We are engaged in exterminating the bourgeoisie as a class. We are not looking for evidence or witness to reveal deeds or words against the Soviet power. First thing you have to ask an arrested person is: To what class does he belong? Where does he come from? What kind of education did he have? What is his occupation? These questions are to decide the fate of the accused. This is the essence of the Red Terror.*[46]

---

[46] Paul M. Johnson, *Modern Times Revised Edition. The World from the Twenties to the Nineties*, New York, Perennial, 1983, pp. 70-71, quoting from Harrison Salisbury, *Black Night; White Snow: Russia's*

III. The Three Campaigns against Amadeo Barletta

As is the case with the life of any individual, that of Amadeo Barletta Barletta is not lacking in situations that might give rise to a legitimate debate on the choices—right or wrong, but understandable—he made at various points in his life. His initial sympathy towards Mussolini's régime, an attitude shared by most Italians in those years, is undoubtedly one of them.

Indeed, his businesses came to be included in the so-called blacklist of Italian and German companies, (Proclaimed List of Certain Blocked Nationals), and he encountered difficulties in obtaining visas to the U.S. due to his having been his country's consul, which today occurs with many Cuban officials due to their connection with the Cuban government and/or the Communist Party. Those collective sanctions against certain foreign nationals were subsequently lifted.

However, as demonstrated by the FBI's own investigations, beyond lending his services as honorary consul for Italy in the Dominican Republic[47], Barletta was

---

Revolution 1905-1971, London, 1978, p. 565.

[47] Vega, op. cit., p. 325. Bernardo Vega states: "The Italian colony did not promote cultural activities tied to its Mother Country. Because of its relatively long sojourn in the country and because of that lack of cohesion, the Italians assimilated into Dominican life

not involved in any criminal act or act of espionage, while the vast majority of Italians, and not a few of those abroad, professed their fanatical support for Il Duce's project.[48]

The fact is that Italian democratic postwar governments bestowed some of Italy's highest honors on Barletta[49]. This reveals the positive light in which this businessman was viewed, who for a few years served

---

much faster than other foreign groups (e.g. the Germans), thus weakening their sense of nationalism. For these reasons the colony's support of Mussolini's fascism was quite tepid. The U.S. Embassy always reported that the Italians made little effort to spread fascist ideas among the Dominicans and did not undertake any kind of spying activities or for aiding their country in the armed conflict".

[48] The FBI report under file 100-1660 drafted by Marion L. Brown on February 5, 1941 declares the investigation of Amadeo Barletta closed, exonerating him of the suspicion of un-American activities. Years later, in June 1945, his name was removed from the list of Italian nationals whose companies were subject to embargo. The documents relative to those FBI investigations make no mention whatsoever of links between the businessman and criminal elements or activities. L. Marion Brown. *Amadeo Barletta. File No. 100-1660*, Miami, Federal Bureau of Investigation, February 5, 1942. National Archives and Records Administration, Maryland.

[49] The Minister of Industry and Commerce awarded him a knighthood in the Order of Merit for Labor, the first Italian not residing in Italy to be so honored. Gronchi. *Cavaliere al Merito del Lavoro No. 1329*. Foglio 121. Volume I, Ministro per l'Industria el il Commercio. Presidente Della Republica. June 2, 1955.

as Italy's consul in two Caribbean countries during part of Mussolini's time in power. Of particular significance is the case of the "Order of the Star for Italian Solidarity", of which Winston Churchill was the fifteenth recipient[50] and Amadeo Barletta the sixteenth. As for the knighthood in the "Order of Merit for Labor", Barletta was the first Italian to receive it who had been living outside his country for many years.

The attacks launched against the reputation of this businessman of Italian descent had, however, little to do with the legitimate debate that historians could argue in regards to Barletta's closeness to Mussolini's régime.

The importance of a detailed analysis of the accusations against this and other businessmen goes beyond the moral obligation of protecting the image of the victims. Their personal honor and that of the coun-

---

[50] Gli Affari Esteri. *Ordine della Stella della Solidarietà Italiana No. 16*, Presidente Della Repubblica Italiana, November 18, 1952. The "Order of the Star for Italian Solidarity" is a national order created in 1947 by the first president of the Italian Republic, Enrico De Nicola, to recognize expatriate or foreign civilians and military personnel who had made an outstanding contribution to Italy's reconstruction. The Order had different classes. Barletta received it for the first time on December 18, 1948 (Record No. 9); the one he received in 1952, Record No. 16, was the Order's highest class. Record No. 15 corresponded to Winston Churchill.

try's republican history are now interconnected by propaganda trying to present itself as historiography in order to denigrate the honor of both.

First Campaign against Amadeo Barletta

Over the last fifty years, the figure of Amadeo Barletta has been attacked through three campaigns coordinated and/or backed by the Cuban government. The first (1960) aimed to justify the seizure of Barletta's properties, in particular his newspaper and television station, based solely on the justification then accepted under law for a confiscation: to have become rich under the protection of Batista's dictatorship. It was on this point alone that the accusations were centered.

At the time, civil war had spread throughout the island. The anticommunist rebellion came to have thousands of insurgents, in addition to insurgent headquarters in three provinces. In that context, the government urgently needed a TV station with national coverage, such as *Telemundo*, and a newspaper with the same level of coverage, such as *El Mundo*, in order to disseminate its war propaganda. To wrest them away from Barletta, the media had to portray him as a Batista supporter.

Barletta, however, never made money under the sponsorship of Fulgencio Batista and Zaldívar in Cuba; his business interests and properties were affected more than once and considerably so by Batista. No Batista government employee or family member had anything to do with Barletta's businesses, nor did Barletta receive financing from government institutions under Batista's dictatorial régime. The Customs Administrator under the Batista régime always denied Barletta the exemptions to which he was entitled according to the law of 1957 so that his company assemblers could import parts. As described by Barletta in his plea of March 22, 1960 before Cuba's Accounts Tribunal, "Far from my businesses enjoying the protection of the Batista régime, what I always encountered were difficulties and even open hostility".[51]

The land Barletta acquired on the outskirts of Havana (Boyeros) was purchased between August and September 1951, prior to Batista's coup on March 10, 1952, so the urban development subsequent to its purchase could not constitute as evidence of collusion with the Batista régime. Equally false were the accusations that Barletta had evaded taxes in 1957, as detailed in the plea he submitted against the confiscation of his assets, not to mention ironic, since the very same revolution that had called on businessmen to not pay taxes

---

[51] Amadeo Barletta Barletta, *Apelación al Tribunal de Cuentas. Expediente 3-2-8884*, Ministry for the Recovery of Misappropriated Assets, Dr. Lázaro Ginebra. Colegio de Abogados de La Habana, March 22, 1960.

until the tyranny fell was now intending to bring Barletta to trial for that very act.

Nor did Barletta collaborate in any persecutions by Batista's political repression units. On the contrary, there are testimonials to the effect that he even hired people linked to the communist party, such as the humorist Marcos Behmaras (whose contract included the intentional payment of an additional amount that was appropriated by the Popular Socialist Party). His only transactions with the Cuban government consisted in the sale of products from his companies (mostly General Motors vehicles) at competitive prices. Although the Supreme Court had already ruled in his favor in 1956 and ordered that a building belonging to him and confiscated by Batista in 1942 be returned, the dictator fled Cuba in January 1959 without complying with the judgment.

The newspaper *El Mundo*, owned by Amadeo Barletta, always maintained a critical editorial line towards the government and favored a non-violent solution to the national crisis. Personalities such as Raúl Roa, Carlos Lechuga, Manuel Bisbé and other prominent revolutionaries worked there.

The accusations made by the newspaper *Revolución* in the days prior to the expropriation of Barletta's properties based on his alleged relationship with

Trujillo served the same purpose of helping to create a negative public opinion at the time his properties were seized, but the accusations were just as ridiculous. Amadeo Barletta was never an associate of Trujillo's (or of his family), much less his "Consul"; he was, rather, his victim and adversary. In fact, when the tobacco company owned by Barletta competed against the one owned by Trujillo, Dominican consumers were intimidated by insinuations that smoking cigarettes manufactured by the company belonging to the Italian immigrant was equivalent to signaling their opposition to the Trujillo régime, something no one who wished to protect their safety would want to do in those years.

Barletta's conflict with Trujillo, which was never resolved, began in 1930 when Barletta warned President Horacio Vásquez about the coup being engineered by the future dictator-for-life. Trujillo's private archives contain files on Amadeo Barletta that show the dictator kept tabs on him wherever he went (Argentina, Cuba, and the United States). Barletta kept in touch with and provided financial aid to prominent Dominican exiles, such as of Dr. Juan Bosch whom he helped during the time the latter lived in Cuba, so that when Bosch was elected president, the grateful Dominican offered Barletta's son the coveted post of ambassador in Washington, an offer that was declined.

Second Attack against Barletta

The second strike against Amadeo Barletta was in the form of a severe newspaper publication in 1971, this time a lengthy article on the ideological pages of the newspaper *Granma*. It was, in fact, a reprisal for the effectiveness of the denunciation by his son, Amadeo Barletta Jr., at the Inter American Press Association's (IAPA) annual meeting regarding the situation of the press in Cuba. The article was signed by Pedro Luis Padrón under the headline "Amadeo Barletta, representative in Cuba of the businesses of the Yankee *Cosa Nostra* gang".[52]

Needless to say that had the least bit of evidence been found in 1960 of a connection between Barletta and organized crime when the Cuban authorities meticulously inspected his offices and audited his accounting books—the audit took place more "informally" over a weekend in January 1960, and then officially and definitively in February of that year—it would have become the focus of attention in both the newspaper campaign against him and in the charges leveled against him by the Ministry for the Recovery of Misappropriated Assets.

---

[52] Pedro Luis Padrón. "Amadeo Barletta, representante en Cuba de los negocios de la pandilla yanqui 'Cosa Nostra'", *Granma*, March 31, 1971.

However, it was not until 1971 that the official mouthpiece of Cuba's Communist Party took on the responsibility of accusing him of being a "mobster", dismissing the denunciations articulated before the IAPA by his son as to the absence of freedom of the press in Cuba. The use of the pejorative term in the article coincided with the international success of Mario Puzo's novel *The Godfather*, which could very well lead one to suppose that, on this occasion, the journalist deemed the use of it to be an effective propaganda tool for denigrating the Barlettas' integrity.

Third Character Assassination Attempt against Amadeo Barletta

The third assault on Barletta's image began in the context of the Fourth Communist Party Congress in 1991, the first important political event after the drug trafficking scandal of the summer of 1989 involving Cuban military institutions. This time, the attacks against Barletta were in reality a collateral element of a larger official objective: to make the Republic of Cuba prior to 1959 seem like a state controlled by the international mafia.

This third wave of attacks began with the writings of Enrique Cirules, and for the first time, an attempt was made to dress them up in academic robes. This sustained campaign—now bolstered by the internet—

has disseminated the message through exploited participants and other innocents and has included the most defamatory falsehoods about Amadeo Barletta.

I have confirmed that the documents quoted by writers such as Enrique Cirules as incriminatory evidence against Amadeo Barletta do not mention him, nor do they prove Barletta's alleged links to the mafia. To back up his arguments, Cirules uses the technique of quoting certain documental sources that in turn reference other sources, thereby discouraging the ordinary reader from following up on them. Any reader who was to track back to the original source would realize that the documentation to which the evidence against Barletta is attributed contains no such evidence. When the primary document on which Cirules bases his allegations is located, it either makes no reference whatsoever to Barletta, or it does not back up the assertion the writer is trying to prove. The late and distinguished Cuban historian Manuel R. Moreno Fraginals always insisted on the need to refer to original sources when undertaking research. In this case, his advice was not followed by those who thoughtlessly echoed Cirules's arguments, later reproduced by T. J. English.

Such is the case, for instance, in the references in the book *El Imperio de La Habana* (The Empire of Havana) to Barletta's alleged management of the Mussolini family's assets. On this topic, Enrique Cirules, the book's author, references his own articles in the October 1991 issue of the magazine *Bohemia*; here, in turn, he references the book *La Coletilla* (The Postscript) by Fidel Castro's late ambassador to France, Gregorio Ortega (1989), who when making his allegation does not indicate the source and instead mixes the topic in with a reference to the issue of the *Gaceta Oficial de Cuba* [Official Gazette of Cuba] in which the confiscation of Barletta's assets is published. And when, finally, one goes through the *Gaceta*'s text, nowhere is Mussolini's name mentioned nor is his family even referenced.[53]

For his part, the freelance U.S. writer T. J. English (currently accused of plagiarism by Enrique Cirules), in his allegations about Barletta, cites a document from the Treasury Department of Miami-Dade's Organized Crime Bureau from September 1961, a document that is now extremely difficult to locate because those archives were dispersed. Nevertheless, I was able to obtain a copy—courtesy of Scott M. Deitche, biographer of Santo Trafficante, Jr.—and it turned out to be the Bureau's file on Trafficante, Jr., which contains no mention of Amadeo Barletta.

---

[53] Resolution No. 3027. Ministry for the Recovery of Misappropriated Assets. *Gaceta Oficial*, March 17, 1960. Havana, pp. 6595-6600.

Nor do the dossiers on Banco Atlántico make any such mention. These dossiers are stored in Cuba's National Archives—very difficult for Cubans and foreigners to access—and are persistently cited by Cirules in his book as evidence of the links between the mafia and this Barletta-owned bank[54], though they do not go beyond stating the administrative vulnerabilities or errors pointed out by auditors during the routine yearly audits conducted by the Banco Nacional of all financial entities. These audits were subsequently declared by Banco Atlántico as having been resolved. An examination of all these records via the photocopies in my possession shows that the errors indicated within them were all addressed, and the bank's final evaluation was satisfactory.

These routine audits never suggested sanctions against Barletta's Banco Atlántico, although other financial entities were audited, which called for the resignation of their directors, as had occurred at several Cuban banks in the fifties. The Banco Hispano Cubano, an institution with close to USD $8 million in deposits and with direct links to Marta Fernández, Batista's wife, and to José López Vilaboy, a strawman for the dictator, who together held 80% of the shares, was au-

---

[54] Enrique Cirules. *El imperio de la Habana*. Chapter VII. "El lavado de dinero", Havana, Cuba: Casa de las Américas, 1993, pp. 175-187.

dited on 10 September 1957 for gross irregularities, and its sale was ordered in July 1958. These actions, which occurred during the most repressive year of Batista's dictatorship, call into question Cirules's assessment that irregularities found by Banco Nacional's auditors at financial entities were resolved with a conspiratorial "slap on the back" between the government and the business class. The allegation of official favoritism towards Banco Atlántico lacks evidence and is unfounded.

Banco Atlántico's official documentation also lacks any evidence to show that Barletta even had a business or personal relationship with the financial sector (tourism/gambling) to which mafia constituents in Cuba were linked. None of his shareholders or creditors had a criminal record, nor did any of them have links to the tourism, hotel, and casino industries.

After more than a dozen interviews, and consulting numerous archives (in addition to painstaking research, through third parties, within Cuba's National Archives) and looking over dozens of books and original documents, I was unable to find a single piece of evidence regarding Amadeo Barletta that incriminates him in the alleged charges.

Particularly valuable during these inquiries was the testimony of the principal biographers of Santo

Trafficante, Jr. (Scott M. Deitche) and Meyer Lansky (Robert Lacey)[55], as well as the testimony of Gordon Wilson, the main person in charge of the historic archives of Miami-Dade County's Organized Crime Bureau.[56] All of them devoted many years to their investigations of these individuals and assured me they never came across the name of Amadeo Barletta in any of the thousands of documents they inspected, nor did they hear it mentioned by the many witnesses they interviewed.

I was also unable to find anything incriminating toward Barletta in the following places: the National Archives of Cuba; the National Palace Archives in Santo Domingo; the *Generalísimo*'s Private Archives (APN-APG), Santo Domingo; the National Archives, Department of State, Maryland; the General Motors archives, Denver; the archives of the Organized Crime Bureau, Miami-Dade County; the Barletta family's personal archives, Santo Domingo; the Cuban Heritage Collection, University of Miami; the Florida Interna-

---

[55] See Robert Lacey, *Little Man: Meyer Lansky and the Gangster Life.* (Little Brown & Company. Canada. 1991) and Scott M. Deitche, *The Silent Don: The Criminal Underworld of Santo Trafficante Jr.* (Barricade Books Inc., United States, 2009).

[56] Wilson's website contains part of that documentation: **http://cuban-exile.com/doc_051-075/doc0073.html**

tional University Library; and the Mary Ferrell Foundation Collection.

I discovered nothing incriminating Amadeo Barletta in the files on him turned over to me by the CIA, the FBI and the U.S. military intelligence service under the Freedom of Information Act (FOIA). Nor was there any mention of him in the Kefauver Commission hearings referred to by the newspaper *Granma* in 1971. Nor does his file at the National Archives, Maryland (including a biographical reference drafted by the U.S. Embassy in Havana in February 1957 a propos of a visa application) contain any reference to a mafia connection.[57]

In a contextualized explanation, both Robert Lacey and Scott M. Deitche, experts on mafia-related topics and on the lives of Lansky and Santo Trafficante in particular, mentioned the reason why they dismissed the

---

[57] It is important to note that this document from February 1957 on Amadeo Barletta drafted at the U.S. Embassy in Cuba by Advisor Vinton Chapin makes no mention of any link between the Italian businessman and criminal elements or activities, just as neither is there any indication of this influential embassy's being cognizant of special links between Barletta and the Batista régime. Vinton Chapin, *Dispatch No. 749. Biographical Information Concerning Amadeo Barletta*. American Embassy in Havana, May 10, 1957, *Ref. Memorandum A-171, File 101.21/5-1057*, February 1, 1957. National Archives and Records Administration, Maryland.

argument concerning the existence of organized mafia "families" in Cuba—which is not the same as to say mafia presence in business dealings—and the allegation that banks were used to "launder money", the source of which was, in fact, legal, since it came from gambling.

Of particular interest is the contribution by Robert Lacey, the only Lansky biographer given access by Israel to the U.S. government's complete dossier on this individual. Through the FOIA, Lacey requested access to the dossiers on Meyer Lansky at various U.S. agencies, and after a certain amount of time, a dossier was handed to him filled with blacked-out sections, making it useless for his purposes.

The indefatigable biographer then travelled to Tel Aviv and submitted a request to the Israeli authorities for access to whatever they had on the subject. To his surprise, the Israelis also handed over the complete U.S. dossier that was sent to them by Washington, accompanying its request that Israel not grant Israeli citizenship to Lansky when he applied for it.

The contents of these files were zealously compiled by all U.S. government agencies, since it was their opportunity to persuade Tel Aviv not to grant Lansky citizenship.

According to Lacey, the files take up more than three linear feet of space, equivalent to two filing cabinet drawers. Lacey indicated that the folders were filled with telegrams, official internal memos, surveillance reports, as well as newspaper articles carefully cut out and added to documents described as "fact sheets". Not one of them mentions Amadeo Barletta nor his alleged leadership of a "mafia family" in Cuba.[58] It should be noted that Lacey also travelled to Cuba to research Lansky's activities, where he reviewed old archives from the Riviera Hotel and others pertinent to his investigation. These also made no reference whatever to Amadeo Barletta or to the legend that Cirules attributes to him of a supposed association with Lansky and other mobsters.

In the opinion of Lacey, Deitche, and the Colombian historian Sáenz Rovner, the huge profits from gambling did not entail any risk, given that gambling was a legal activity, which is why no one wishing to remain in that sector would imperil the enormous rates of return by becoming involved in parallel risky operations, such as drug trafficking.

Another relevant fact is that ever since Amadeo Barletta founded Santo Domingo Motors in the Domin-

---

[58] Lacey. Op. cit., pp. 314-315.

ican Republic, the history of the creation of his initial capital and its subsequent growth has been documented, and nowhere is there any indication of a connection with organized crime or of links to sectors such as tourism and casinos.[59]

Had there been any criminal connection or any spying for the Axis powers, it would have been detected during the aforementioned detailed investigation of Barletta and his finances undertaken by the FBI between July 1941 and February 1942. The investigation was conducted in Cuba, as well as in New York and Buenos Aires, where Barletta lived after resigning his post as Italy's Honorary Consul in Havana. The investigation came to an end when the special agent in charge of the case concluded that the Italian businessman was not involved in un-American activities,[60] a

---

[59] I was able to access the company's archives, as well as Amadeo Barletta's personal archives, courtesy of his family who also allowed me to copy some of the more relevant documents to aid in this investigation. I was able to go over the Minutes Book of Shareholders' Meetings from 1920 to 1962, which show the normal growth of a company that suffered several setbacks (hurricane San Zenón in 1930, and World War II). There is no relevant or suspicious information in terms of a sudden increase in capital or hidden shareholders.

[60] Brown, op. cit. Another FBI document dated February 16, 1942 drafted by H. H. Calkies contains a detailed reference to various deposit accounts, stock, and bond securities in companies owned by Barletta that were blocked by the embargo then in effect against

concept that in the United States has been flexible enough to range from the activities of a potential spy to organized crime.

I still have an extensive collection of photocopies of all the relevant information found in the files, the tape-recordings of interviews conducted throughout the investigation, and the correspondence with certain Cuban and foreign experts on the topics addressed. I also conducted complimentary research on the origins and history of Banco Atlántico, via access to all available documentation in the National Archives of Cuba.

What Could Have Motivated the Campaign Begun in 1989?

The analysis of this campaign against Amadeo Barletta compels the researcher to adhere to the same methodological rules used by historiographers when assessing sources in order to determine the value of the articles promoting Cirules's work, which have been posted on various websites.

---

companies owned by Italian citizens. Nowhere is there a reference to the possible dubious origin of these assets or to any suspicious activity regarding the businessman's finances. *H. H. Calkies, Amadeo Barletta. File No. 100-15049*, New York, Federal Bureau of Investigation, February 18, 1942.

Who is making these allegations? What is his or her intellectual and/or political background? What could motivate someone or several people to foster this viewpoint now? Is the case one of a concerted effort, given that the same arguments are repeated without subjecting them to analysis with the aim of imposing them as "common sense"? Can the source be in a position such as to have access to that information and really know what he or she is talking about? What genuine access to the aforementioned data could the source have had? Do his or her assertions show biased or rhetorical language?

These general questions lead to other specific ones about this case. Why is this new defamatory effort taking place almost two decades after the 1971 broadside was printed in *Granma* in response to Barletta Jr.'s denunciations at the IAPA? Is this the work of a single individual who is leveling these accusations from a lack of professional rigor? Are we facing a new chapter in the campaigns previously organized against this person? If this is so, what is the motivation, and what are the objectives this time around? I put forward the opinion that beyond the role personally played, wittingly or not, by Cirules, his work's warm reception and the support provided by government institutions for its dissemination was given in pursuit of an objective over and above the goal of once again denigrating the person of Amadeo Barletta.

There are reasons to suppose that the intention behind the dissemination of Cirules's writings on this topic was to promote his argument that the drug-trafficking scandal uncovered in 1989—which concluded with the execution by firing squad of General Arnaldo Ochoa and other senior military commanders—was an isolated and exceptional incident in the revolutionary process, whereas all the prosperity of the Cuban business class under capitalism came from an alliance with the mafia, the U.S. intelligence services, and Cuban politicians of that era.

In propaganda terms, Cirules's articles and writings since 1989 objectively served the Cuban government's need to justify the revelations that shocked public opinion in Cuba and internationally that same year regarding the relationship between Fidel Castro's government and drug-trafficking.[61]

---

[61] Certainly the drug-trafficking scandal has constituted one of the most serious legitimacy crises faced by Fidel Castro's authority. Since the days of the civil war against the social-democratic elements of the anti-Batista coalition, never had there been a greater purge of senior revolutionary party members. In addition to the small group of Ministry of the Interior (MININT) and Armed Revolutionary Forces (FAR as per the initials in Spanish) officers who were either executed or imprisoned, a complete reorganization

It is especially curious that between the 4th and 25th of October 1991, coinciding with the celebration of the Fourth Cuban Communist Party Congress, the magazine *Bohemia* prominently published a series of four articles by Cirules on drug-trafficking and the mafia in the republican era.[62]

This Congress was the first held by the Cuban communists after the drug-trafficking scandal of mid-1989 and the sweeping purge of officers at the Ministry of the Interior (MININT) in the wake of those events. In the articles published in *Bohemia*, Cirules already mentions the book he was "working on" (*El imperio de la Habana*" or "The Empire of Havana") on the always best-selling topic of the mafia.[63]

---

of MININT took place in which dozens of senior officers were removed from their posts and/or barred from the institution.

[62] Enrique Cirules, "El imperio de la Habana", *Bohemia*, October 4, 1991; "Operaciones y fraudes", *Bohemia*, October 11, 1991; "Los negocios de don Amleto", *Bohemia*, October 18, 1991; "Traficante: la era de la cocaína", *Bohemia*, October 25, 1991.

[63] The topic of the mafia undoubtedly drives book sales. The United States in particular is fascinated by its gangsters, which guarantees success to any author offering new stories about them. They are an indivisible part of American pop culture as stated by writers who are authorities on the subject, such as Robert Lacey and Scott M. Deitche.

Cirules's professional career has been closely linked to Cuba's Armed Revolutionary Forces (FAR as per the initials in Spanish). When the FAR encouraged government institutions to apply an anti-cultural policy that subsequently came to be known as the "grey five-year period" (1970-1975), Cirules was appointed director of one of the principal magazines of the time — *Revolución y Cultura* (Revolution and Culture) — which he edited during that terrible period (1971-1975).[64]

While writing for the FAR's newspaper (*Bastión*), Cirules visited Colombia in 1988[65], allegedly on a private tour, returning again in the summer of 1989, which coincided with the outbreak of the drug-trafficking scandal in Cuba that had been under investigation since the previous year.

On that second trip, Cirules remained in Colombia for three months, this time accompanied by his wife.[66] On his return, *Bastión* published a series of Sunday articles on drug-trafficking written by him, and aimed at implicitly demonstrating that the drug-trafficking scourge was global and the recent scandal in Cuba was

---

[64] Ricardo L. Hernández, "La vida literaria en la Cuba actual: sus revistas", La Palabra del Hombre, 1988, pp. 39-46.

[65] Enrique Cirules, op.cit., Introduction, p.9.

[66] Ibid.

not part of an endemic structural phenomenon within the Cuban system as was the case in other parts of the world.[67]

In 1991, as previously stated, the Cuban writer published four weekly articles on the topic in the magazine *Bohemia*, which were the prelude to his subsequent books *El Imperio de la Habana* (The Empire of Havana) in 1993 and *La Vida Secreta de Meyer Lansky en La Habana* (The Secret Life of Meyer Lansky in Havana) in 2004. In these articles, he incorporated the figure of the businessman Amadeo Barletta into his recounting of the mafia presence in Cuba. This time the assault on the dignity of Amadeo Barletta was collateral damage rather than the articles' main objective. "Nothing personal", as the central character in Mario Puzo's *The Godfather* would say. The Cuban writer seemingly decided in 1989 that he was free to do what he saw fit with the reputation of Barletta, who had passed away in 1975, in order to freely construct his fantastic plot about a republic completely under the thumb of the

---

[67] In the Acknowledgements to his book *El Imperio de la Habana*, Cirules states that it was Juan Agüero Gómez, then *Bastión*'s editor in chief, who in 1989, on his return from Colombia, published the articles mentioned here, which the Cuban author wrote with his wife. It was also Agüero, as Cirules recounts in the Acknowledgements, who encouraged him to write a book on the topic of the mafia in Cuba in the pre-revolutionary era. Ibid, p. 355.

Italian-American mafia of which General Fulgencio Batista was a sort of glorified employee. In his narrative, Amadeo Barletta is introduced as the alleged leader of one of the four (nonexistent) mafia families that, in his opinion, controlled the country's destiny.

I, however, after conducting more than a dozen interviews, consulting numerous archives (in addition to thoroughly researching the documentation in Cuba's own National Archives), examining dozens of books, and analyzing hundreds of original documents in official and private archives in the United States and the Dominican Republic, was unable to find a single piece of evidence incriminating Amadeo Barletta in any way or corroborating the alleged accusations against him.

In short, once subjected to scrutiny, Enrique Cirules's and T. J. English's spectacular allegations regarding Amadeo Barletta proved to be completely lacking in any factual evidence.

IV. The methodological weaknesses of Enrique Cirules

In the previous paragraphs, I reviewed the groundlessness of the accusations leveled against Amadeo Barletta at various times. Next, I will focus on demonstrating a series of methodological weaknesses in Enrique Cirules's writings on this subject.

An analysis of both of Cirules's books on mafia activities in Cuba—*The Empire of Havana* and *The Secret Life of Meyer Lansky in Havana: The Mafia in Cuba*—shows that they present a series of problems, among which the following are notable:

a)   *Faulty management of primary sources, particularly in the case of his star witness, the late Jaime Casielles, and proposing arbitrarily unanimous interpretations of ambiguous facts.*

At no time does Cirules show any inclination to conduct an "internal criticism" analysis of the testimony given, so he says, by Jaime Casielles. The reader is entitled to expect Cirules to ask, in respect of his interviewee, questions such as: How long has it been since the events occurred, and what capacity for involuntary distortion could Casielles have exhibited when recounting them? Was Casielles truly in a position to know or directly witness each and every one of the events he narrates, given that he was, as described by himself, a simple valet? Did he feel under pressure/forced/encouraged to provide a certain tendentious version of events and individuals to Cirules because he knew it was what was expected of him?

Cirules does not ask his witnesses the classic questions posed by investigators: Who? What? Where? When? Why?

Historians need to ask themselves a series of questions about their sources: Who gathered the information? Did they have first-hand access to the facts? What did they have to say about the topics being investigated? How far in time or distance were they from the events? What do the witnesses have to say about the facts and participants being investigated? When was the testimony regarding the facts taken down: immediately following the events or years later? Why is a particular source willing to provide his or her testimony? Are there motivations leading them to be prejudiced in their interpretations?

The manner in which Cirules processed Jaime Casielles's testimony, who for several months in 1958 was Meyer Lansky's valet in Cuba, is especially interesting when evaluating various sets of Cirules arguments and, in particular, his statements regarding Amadeo Barletta.

To start with, one need only point out that it is quite hard to believe that a person as extraordinarily reserved as Meyer Lansky would give access to sensitive information regarding his business to someone like Jaime Casielles, whom he had met one month previously through a third party, and had just started working as a mere valet during Lansky's time in Cuba.

In regards to the references Casielles makes to Barletta, there is not a single one that would enable one to deduce a connection between Amadeo Barletta and Lansky or his circle. There is no testimony by Casielles in Cirules's books in which Lansky's former valet says he saw Barletta embrace Lansky, or that he drove his employer to meetings with the Italian businessman, or that he overheard a conversation about their joint business deals. In fact, the only two anecdotes Casielles said he recalled regarding Barletta, which Cirules cites, could be interpreted the other way around.

One of them was the gesture of disapproval that Casielles "thought" he saw Lansky make when Lansky was informed that an apartment had been rented in the Barletta-owned Ambar Motors building to set up a school for croupiers as part of the investment process in an activity as legal as gambling was at the time.[68] The school did indeed use to be at that location, in addition to another one that was located in the Dental Building for several months and operated without incident. Approval by the tenants and the collection of the rent for the space were not the responsibility of Amadeo Barletta, but of the building's assistant manager Luis Allen.[69] The Ambar Motors building housed the offices of the Canadian embassy and of several highly reputable law firms. The building's security would not have advised renting space to underworld elements that would be involved in illegal activities within the building.[70]

The other anecdote recounted by Casielles to Cirules took place during the inauguration of the Habana Riviera Hotel, when Casielles recalls witnessing the arrival of the sugar magnate Julio Lobo accompanied by Amadeo Barletta, and seeing Lobo leaving Barletta's side to briefly greet

---

[68] Cirules, op. cit., p. 80.

[69] Luis Allen, interview with the author, Coral Gables, Florida, December 13, 2009.

[70] Ibid.

Lansky in the lobby.[71] The brief greeting between Lobo and Meyer does not necessarily have any sinister significance. The fact is that the only specific thing attested to by Casielles is that Amadeo Barletta never approached or greeted Lansky.

In both cases, the manner in which Cirules tries to interpret and magnify his version of events is very unprofessional for a historian. His approach is more nearly that of conspiracy theorists[72], whose maxim is "if reality doesn't coincide with theory, so much the worse for reality."

In line with his theory, the Cuban writer assumes that if Barletta avoided Lansky, it was to conceal a relationship with the gangster and not because there was simply no link whatsoever between

[71] Enrique Cirules. *La vida secreta de Meyer Lansky en La Habana: la Mafia en Cuba,* Havana, Editorial de Ciencias Sociales, 2004, p. 140.

[72] Michael Barkun, professor of political science at Syracuse University and a specialist in millenarian movements, the radical right and terrorism, believes the essence of conspiracy theories stems from the belief that the forces of evil and external elements dominate history based on three principles: Nothing occurs by accident. Nothing is what it seems. Everything is connected. Michael Barkun, *A Culture of Conspiracy: Apocalyptic Visions in Contemporary America,* Berkeley and Los Angeles, California, University of California Press, 2006.

them. If, in addition, Lansky disliked the idea of renting space in the Ambar Motors building, according to Cirules it was because he did not want to "put Barletta on the spot", not because he, perhaps, did not like the building or because he thought it preferable to choose a place adjacent to the one already being rented at 23 and L streets, in El Vedado district, or even because being Jewish,[73] he would not be too fond of someone like Amadeo, who had been Italian consul during part of Mussolini's time in power, and who, by the way, unceremoniously crushed the Sicilian mafia.[74]

Cirules makes historical characters think and speak according to how he has decided events occurred. A typical example is the previously mentioned case when Casielles said he deduced a

[73] Lacey, op. cit. For further information on Lansky's activities against the Nazis, see Chapter 7, "I will help you. It's Patriotism".

[74] Mussolini was perennial enemy of the mafia, ever since his first trip to Sicily when the *capo* at the time tried to boast that only he could offer Mussolini protection during his visit. Il Duce took this as a humiliation and on his return to Rome, successfully declared "battle to the death" on the mafia, for which the latter never forgave him. For further information, see "Foreign News: Mafia Trial", *Time*, October 24, 1927; and "ITALY: Mafia Scotched", *Time*, January 23, 1928.

gesture of disapproval by Lansky when told of the rental of space in the Ambar Motors building to set up a school for croupiers. Casielles himself says that he is not absolutely sure, but that it seemed to him that Lansky disapproved of the idea, whereas Cirules prefers to present the gesture as a matter of fact to show that Lansky was indeed displeased, and then assumes that the reason was the need to seemingly keep a distance from Barletta.[75]

b)   *In order to substantiate his contentions, he attributes statements and data to sources or individuals who do not mention the matter in the original sources.*

Cirules makes contentions he supports with quotes from documents whose contents do not back up what he is asserting. As previously stated, such is the case of his quoting from the book *La Coletilla* in order to assert that Barletta managed the Mussolini family's assets.[76] The truth is that the book's author, Gregorio Ortega, in turn refers readers to Resolution 3027 of 8 March of

---

[75] Ibid.

[76] Indeed, it is a well-known fact that the Mussolini family lived in reduced circumstances after Il Duce's death.

the Ministry for the Recovery of Misappropriated Assets, in which anyone can confirm upon reading it that it contains no reference to any link between Barletta and the mafia or Mussolini's family.[77]

c)   *In his account, he mixes personal opinions with quotes from witness accounts.*

Enrique Cirules uses Jaime Casielles's testimony to back up his theories about the mafia's activities in Cuba, but, despite Casielles's being his main "witness for the prosecution", he doesn't bother to enclose his statements in quotation marks to clearly distinguish them from statements added by him, the writer, thus generating inaccuracies that compound his readers' confusion.

d)   *The absence of a hermeneutical approach that would put the central characters' actions and attitudes into context for their correct interpretation.*

When used out of context, concepts such as "money laundering", "mafia families", "pyramid scheme" and others used by Cirules are confus-

---

[77] Gregorio Ortega, *La Coletilla,* Havana: Editorial Política, 1989, pp. 168-169.

ing and distort the events that occurred in the reality of the 1950s.

It has to be said that claiming Lansky's casinos needed to "launder" their profits is absurd. Here again he uses a term ("money laundering") that has absolutely no connection to Cuban reality in the fifties in regards to activities tied to the gambling businesses of Meyer Lansky, Santo Trafficante Jr. or Amleto Battisti.[78]

Money laundering—as explained to me by three leading mafia experts: Lacey, Deitche, and Sáenz—implies erasing the illegal source of capital. Since gambling was a legal and public activity in pre-revolutionary Cuba, there was no need to

---

[78] The U.S. consulate in Havana conducted an investigation on this topic between December 1941 and April 1942, and, with the information gathered, drafted a report in seven folios of the entire history and all the activities of Amleto Battisti y Lora from his birth in Salto, Uruguay on 9 September 1893. Amleto Battisti controlled the lottery known as *la bolita* (the small ball), the Oriental Park where horse racing took place, the Casino Nacional and the Sevilla Hotel; his diversified investment portfolio also included ownership of a newspaper and stock in another. The report, dated April 15, 1942, is addressed to the Secretary of State in Washington and is signed by Consul General Harold S. Tewell. It does not contain a single mention of Amadeo Barletta. (Tewell, Harold S., *Information Concerning Mr. Amleto Battisti, Havana, Cuba. File 865.20210 Battisti, Amleto/3*. American Consulate General, April 15, 1942.)

"launder" the source.

Nor did the gangsters in Cuba need Barletta's Banco Atlántico to transfer funds to lend support to gambling-related activities (not to "launder" money, which was unnecessary) since Amleto Battisti owned his own bank[79]. Furthermore, if they wanted to evade U.S. taxes by declaring income below their real income to the IRS, the best system was the one in use at the time: suitcases filled with cash personally transported to Miami, Switzerland or elsewhere to be deposited not in bank accounts, but in safety-deposit boxes (this was at a time when customs agencies did not impose any limit on the amount of cash passengers could carry). At various hearings before the U.S. Congress, American gangsters testified that this was the preferred method they used to safeguard the profits from the casinos in Cuba.[80]

---

[79] "Banco de Crédito e Inversiones" in *Los propietarios de Cuba 1958,* Guillermo Jiménez, references to Battisti Lora, Amleto, p. 75.

[80] Michael Woodiwiss, "Transnational Organized Crime: The Strange Career of an American Concept", in *Critical Reflections on Transnational Organized Crime, Money Laundering, and Corruption.* Ed. Margaret E. Beare, Toronto: University of Toronto Press, 2003.

On the other hand, as stated by the Colombian historian, Sáenz Rovner[81], narcotics trafficking through Cuba (where there was minimum consumption) was an activity reserved to small criminal groups of mostly European origin (not the Italian-American mafia), since the profits were inferior to those gained through the gambling business, a legal activity. This is why those who could devote themselves to the casino business did not get involved in illegal dealings that could endanger the "goose that lays the golden eggs". As Sáenz Rovner explains:

> *As demonstrated by the documents in Cuban and U.S. archives, the mafia's businesses in Cuba were centered mainly on casinos and the tourism industry, not, as the Cuban writer Enrique Cirules has claimed, on drug trafficking.[82]*

As explained, Banco Atlántico was audited three times—once a year as established under law for any banking institution—and was never penal-

---

[81] Eduardo Sáenz Rovner, *The Cuban Connection*, Chapel Hill, The University of North Carolina Press, 2008 [translated by Russ Davidson].

[82] Ibid. pp. 7-8.

ized or audited for shady dealings. Whoever questions, as Enrique Cirules does, the quality or honesty of those audits should provide an explanation of the motives behind the Trust Company of Cuba —recognized as one of the most effective and powerful banking institutions in the world at the time— when it acquired Banco Atlántico after subjecting it, as is proper before an acquisition, to a detailed examination.

A note by a bank auditor regarding the need to "keep a close eye on"[83] Banco Atlántico was distorted by Cirules, who gives it a sinister crime-related connotation, despite the auditor's own explanation of the reason for his note: "In regards to its credit policies, well, it's well known that its directors, with few exceptions, are individuals given to daring business deals"[84]. Law 13 of 1948[85] slowed down investment processes be-

---

[83] Sergio Valdés Rodríguez, *Memorándum del Comité de Inspección Bancaria: Dr. J. Martínez Sáenz, Sr. Bernardo Figueredo, Sr. Oswaldo Saura. Re: Banco Atlántico, S.A. Inspección de diciembre 9, 1952*. March 11, 1953. Fondo del Banco Nacional de Cuba. Cuban National Archives.

[84] Ibid.

[85] Joaquín Martínez Sáenz, *Por la independencia económica de Cuba. Mi gestión en el Banco Nacional*, Havana, Editorial Cenit S.A., 1959.

cause the inclination was to guarantee that banks have sufficient liquidity at all times, in case they have to face a sudden crisis such as the one that occurred in 1929. The auditor worried that Barletta's investment boldness—Barletta had a basic education and was a banker with full decision-making powers without a degree in economics—would induce him to risk more capital than was permitted under law at that time.

The connotation of the word *piramidación*[86] (pyramid scheme), used in an auditor's note regarding the companies affiliated with Banco Atlántico, is not the one it has today. It is now used to describe the schemes used by a swindler like Bernard Madoff. This note is the only one in which the term appears from among hundreds of pages containing the auditor's reports on Banco Atlántico. In fact, the auditor was referring to the fact that the bank received funds from its affiliated companies and, without altering its banking principles, reinvested the majority of this capital

---

[86] Miguel Termes, *Memorándum al Comité de Inspección Bancaria. Dr. Felipe Pazos, Dr. J. A. Guerra, Sr. O. Saura. RE: Compañías afiliadas y tenedoras afiliadas del Banco Atlántico, S.A., Fondo del Banco Nacional de Cuba,* Havana, Cuban National Archives.

in expanding its businesses, which was a practice that had been tested by General Motors with its companies, but was a novelty business tactic in Cuba.[87]

The fact is that those same auditors, in their third and final audit[88] of Banco Atlántico, indicated their conformity with the manner in which the administrative weaknesses previously pointed out were being remedied.[89] This final audit issued a rating of "Healthy" to the bank's credit policies, "Normal" to its solvency, "Ample" to its capital reserves and provision, and did not give any of

---

[87] Alfred P. Sloan Jr., *My years with General Motors*, New York: Doubleday, 1963; Allyn Freeman, *The leadership genius of Alfred P. Sloan*, New York, McGraw-Hill, 2005.

[88] Jorge M. Portal, *Memorándum al Comité de Inspección Bancaria: Sres. J. Martínez Sáenz, Bernardo Figueredo y S. Valdés Rodríguez. Resumen del Informe de Inspección al Banco Atlántico, S.A., 8 de diciembre de 1953*. February 9, 1954. Fondo del Banco Nacional de Cuba. Cuban National Archives.

[89] Cirules, in keeping with his viewpoint of a totally corrupt republic with no division of powers, assumes that any fault the auditors of Banco Nacional may have found in a financial institution owned by Barletta was remedied by a few "pats on the back". The reality was very different. Both Banco Nacional and its chairman Dr. Martínez Sáenz were extremely professional and exacting in their work, as has been attested to by Cuban historians specializing in this issue.

the categories analyzed a negative ratings, of which the form provided the following choices to include: Dangerous, Sub-Normal, Unacceptable and Insufficient.

V. Cirules versus the Republic of Cuba

From a professional point of view, it would be easy to dismiss this author, who by his own admission is not a historian, but even if he is not, he should be taken seriously, and it should be demanded of him that he apply the rigor that anyone who ventures into this field should apply out of respect for his or her readers.

I will therefore begin by wholeheartedly agreeing with the distinguished Colombian historian and expert Eduardo Sáenz Rovner when he says in his book *The Cuban Connection* (2008):

> ...*(the) recent works published in Cuba on drug trafficking, such as the studies by Enrique Cirules and Francisco Arias Fernández, portray the pre-1959 island as a haven for official corruption fueled by drug-trafficking, while stating that Batista personally supported the drug traffickers. Nevertheless, there is no empirical evidence that makes it possible to maintain the notion that Batista offered such support in the fifties (....) Cirules's writings are filled with claims and arguments regarding drug traffick-*

*ing and narcotics that are lacking in any empir-
ical evidence and ultimately turn into subjective
political judgments.*[90]

The reason behind the methodological superficiali-
ty of these and other historical studies is not always
related to the inadequate degree of professionalism of
those who produce them. It is the political-ideological
demands governing Cuban historiography's propaganda activities that favor such literature. As noted by
the historian Louis Pérez when referring to works of
this type, "public policy and historical constructions
run parallel to the extent that Havana deliberately
manages to discredit the pre-revolutionary past".[91] I,
too, concur with Pérez's point of view.

It is not this essay's intent to refute Cirules's general argument against the republican period of 1933 to
1958, not because it cannot be challenged, but because
addressing that far-reaching topic exceeds the purposes of this work. It is a topic that deserves to be addressed separately. Suffice it to say that Cirules's claim
that he has contributed a new interpretive paradigm

---

[90] Sáenz Rovner, op. cit., pp.10-12 [Translated back into English]

[91] Louis A. Perez, *Essays on Cuban History: Historiography and
Research*, Gainesville, Florida, University Press of Florida, 1995, p.
147.

with his "findings",[92] which demands the complete revision of everything previously written, is truly as pretentious as it is erroneous. The idea that the inequitable but extraordinarily prosperous Cuban economy of the 1940s and 1950s was underpinned by Havana's casinos—which today would all fit onto a narrow alleyway in Las Vegas, Atlantic City or even Santo Domingo—is deserving of an analysis that goes beyond the limits of this essay.

Narcotics trafficking and consumption in Cuba was very limited and controlled mainly by Europeans. The importance of gambling—legal and lucrative—in which, in addition to Cubans, a few American mobsters were partially involved, was insignificant in the Cuban economy of 1958.

---

[92] Luis Hernández Serrano, "Enrique Cirules: Mis libros no se pueden plagiar impunemente", *Juventud Rebelde*, Havana, March 13, 2010.

http://www.juventudrebelde.cu/cuba/2010-03-13/enrique-cirules-mis-libros-no-se-pueden-plagiar-impunemente/ (Accessed: March 15, 2010)

Luis Hernández Serrano, "Entre la mafia y el plagio", *Juventud Rebelde*, Havana, February 10, 2010.

http://www.juventudrebelde.cu/cuba/2010-02-11/entre-la-mafia-y-el-plagio/ (Accessed: March 15, 2010)

According to the classic book by the eminent geographer and historian Leví Marrero, *Geografía de Cuba* (Geography of Cuba), non-sugar industrial production in 1953 already exceeded the big business of sugar production. Furthermore, 121 of the 161 existing sugar mills in 1958 were owned by Cubans. That year, total U.S. capital investment in Cuba was USD $861 million, barely 14% of a total investment of USD $6 billion. Also, by 1958 Cuban banks controlled 60% of all deposits.[93]

The second obvious issue is that, unlike the offensives against Barletta in 1960 and 1971, the accusations being made this time are not aimed exclusively at him, but at the whole of pre-revolutionary society between 1933 and 1958. The year chosen by Cirules, 1933, as the dividing line indicating the ascent of a "State of a criminal nature" coincides with the moment in which the figure of Sergeant Fulgencio Batista y Zaldívar burst upon the scene in Cuban history.

In Enrique Cirules's own words, the central thesis he sets out to prove in his two books about mafia activities in Cuba is as follows:

---

[93] *Grupo Cubano de Investigaciones Económicas* (Cuban Economic Research Project) at the University of Miami under the direction of José R. Álvarez Díaz, *Un estudio sobre Cuba: colonia, república, experimento socialista: estructura económica, desarrollo institucional, socialismo y regresión,* Miami: University of Miami Press, 1963.

> *The existence in Cuba, prior to the Revolution, of a trilogy that held the real power: financial groups, the mafia, and U.S. special services – all of which, voracious, established a State of a criminal nature in our country, in conformity with the interests of the Havana-Las Vegas clan.*[94]

According to Cirules, his "discoveries" on this topic have led to "…a new understanding of that time, very conscious of the relationship between Cuba and the United States, and, by extension, of its consequences up to the present day. And the about-face represented by the publication of *El imperio de La Habana* (*The Empire of Havana*) in 1993 as it regards the historical analyses of the 25 years prior to the triumph of the Cuban Revolution".[95]

In other words, the author set out to demonstrate in his two books that the Cuban State that existed in the twenty-five years prior to 1959, i.e. since 1933, was controlled by the Sicilian-American mafia in partnership with U.S. intelligence services and local politicians. In my opinion, and in light of what I have already put forth, it would be unfortunate if academi-

---

[94] Hernández Serrano, op. cit.

[95] Ibid.

cians were to echo his arguments without subjecting them to criticism and reinterpreted Cuba's history as of 1933 due to his alleged findings.

From Cirules's viewpoint, which is the Cuban government's official viewpoint, the drug trafficking scandal of 1989 was a *peccadillo*, a minor incident in the purportedly immaculate history of the revolution, which, according to Cirules, was able to quickly "solve" the problem. This was the message of his books, and also, apparently, the message whose transmission was desired by those from within the structures of the Cuban government, who encouraged him to write them and supported the dissemination of his work. The way in which the mechanisms for spreading his message functioned, in order to create a snowball with traits similar to those of viral marketing, is the typical one used by official propaganda campaigns targeted overseas.

VI. Character Assassination Online

There are significant problems with the accusations against Barletta subsequent to the 1989 drug trafficking scandal involving the Cuban state.

One is that they are disseminated via multiple media outlets, in particular newspapers and the Internet, which draw on material with academic pretensions, such as Cirules's books.

Given the control the Cuban government exercises over publications, publishing houses, literary prizes, and access to the press, as well as the restrictive circumstances in which the island's intellectual output takes place, it is always striking when all of these institutions coordinate to favor an author and agree to disseminate his works. This is not to say that everyone favored in this way can be suspected of directly serving the interests of the State. There are academicians and writers who have produced exceptional and unquestionably valuable work that has earned them well-deserved awards, but whose subject matter does not compel them to infringe upon the sacred truths of official ideology. Termed "noble topics" by the authorities, they are those that avoid all areas of interpretive conflict with the island's government. But when the topic is clearly political, touching on matters that are important to the Cuban government, and it receives a disproportionate amount of exposure in official media, there are reasons to believe this is not a casual occurrence, given the circumstances of the island's intellectual output.

A study of the promotional activities surrounding Cirules's work shows that they followed the classic formula (used in Cuba in official propaganda campaigns) of constructing concentric circles to multiply the message's reach.

In this case, the first circle draws on the works of Cirules, amplified by their receiving national "awards" from government institutions, as well as positive mentions by literary journalists or critics from the official press, and laudatory comments from cultural sector government officials and government-controlled websites.

The second circle is constituted by "ideological fellow travelers" (foreign journalists, literary critics, academicians, politicians, artists) in various countries who sympathize with the Cuban government and echo — oftentimes on their own initiative, or else in response to Havana's request or suggestion—the opinions issued by the first circle. Because these individuals are foreigners living in democratic countries, the message gains more credibility.

The third circle crowns this effort when the campaign's hypotheses are adopted by people outside the Cuban government's control and influence, who have honestly believed the message and spontaneously begun repeating it and broadening its reach.[96]

---

[96] This seems to have been the case of the freelance writer T. J. English, who in his book *Havana Nocturne,* uncritically adopts the theses posited by Cirules, but does not thereby seem to be responding "organically" to the campaign sponsored by the Cuban government promoting them. To the extent that he was an exponent within that third circle of gullible individuals, nobody in

An analysis of the presence of Cirules's works in national and international media shows that the Cuban government has successfully been able to construct and foster these three circles in order to promote the works.

VII. Conclusions

My research was unable to find any basis for the negative statements regarding Amadeo Barletta. I decided not to articulate any preliminary hypothesis that could contaminate the search, whereby the gathering and processing of information that would make me veer in one direction or another. In regards to the accusations leveled against Barletta, throughout the course of my research my aim was always not to reject them in ad-

---

Havana protested his book. In fact, his publication by an organization unrelated to the promoters of the intentional discrediting of Amadeo Barletta and of republican society in general, was an indication of the campaign's success being achieved. However, they later suddenly decided to discredit English for allegedly plagiarizing Cirules. This is rather ironic because what these character assassination campaigns accomplish is precisely the mechanical and unthinking repetition of the defamatory message. When I confronted English with the lack of evidence against Amadeo Barletta, and the lack of any mention of his name in some of the documents and testimony cited by him and by Cirules, he gave evasive answers and to date has not provided any counter evidence or granted a request for an interview. I am still in possession of my correspondence with English.

vance, but to corroborate them by means of the documents upon which it is said the charges laid at his door are based.

My investigation led me to the following conclusions:

1) From the very start of the revolutionary process of 1959, officially organized smear campaigns played a prominent role in discrediting adversaries and legitimizing various types of actions taken against them. In the case of the business community, and even in that of the market as a wealth-generating mechanism, these smear campaigns continued until all assets had been expropriated — not just those owned by the tycoons, but by all self-employed workers. From the outset, the accusations made against important businessmen in order to expropriate them were, as a rule, part of a general character assassination campaign against the business sector, carried out using every possible means controlled by the government in order to gradually begin the dismantling process of all small, medium, and large entrepreneur, and of the market, a process that culminated in March 1968.

2) We must differentiate between the plurality of the approaches of historians — who in their activi-

ties start with different ideologies and interpretive paradigms—and the falsehoods deliberately generated and disseminated by the state propaganda machine. Among the latter, the destruction of the reputation of the republican era, its institutions, and its most outstanding personalities has been an ongoing effort by the Cuban government for half a century. The contention that republican history was under the control of the mafia is an ideological construct. Even though one can reconstruct the history of the presence of prominent international mafia elements in Cuba, the country's history cannot possibly be reduced to nothing more than the mafia's history on the island. Nor is it a reality that the existing "evils" on the island were imported. Gambling as a social problem existed from Colonial times, and gangsterism in Cuba was linked first and foremost to the use of violence in national politics.

3)   It is impossible to assert the existence of "mafia families" in Cuba. Robert Lacey, Meyer Lansky's biographer, explained to me (January 9, 2010) that he found a great deal of evidence of Lansky's and other Americans' involvement in running Havana's casinos in the fifties, "but nothing to justify the use of the term *mafia families,* suggesting violence, intimidation, and murder. The rea-

son why Batista welcomed Lansky and others was because they did not use those techniques" (in Cuba).

Bearing in mind Lacey's remarks, it can be said that the use of the concept *mafia families* is much more in line with the type of political gangsterism that ran rampant in Cuba in the forties. The continuous personal attacks and battles royal among rival groups—such as the one known as "*Los Sucesos de Orfila*" (The Events on Orfila) that occurred in Havana on 15 September 1947—became so serious that in 1948 President Carlos Prío approved an Anti-Gangsterism Act. The topic of political gangsterism in Cuba exceeds the scope of this investigation, but that type of gangsterism was more important and influential in the island's history than the considerable yet limited economic impact of mafia activities associated with gambling and tourism.

4) The specific attacks against Amadeo Barletta show all the signs of the twisted and indirect way in which official slander is constructed. His history as a businessman, however, far from being associated with questionable financial activities or sources, was an exceptional example of tenacity, hard work, innovation, and foresight that can serve well as inspiration for other businessmen

and immigrants. Few people ever have to face five major setbacks during the course of their existence and are then able to recover without being paralyzed by despondency or rancor.

Barletta lost almost all his capital and was able to raise it again when hurricane San Zenon slammed into the Dominican Republic in 1930. Then, in 1935, Trujillo audited his companies when he arrested and tortured him for several weeks. In 1941, Batista confiscated part of his property in Cuba, some of which was never returned at the end of World War II, even though the courts ruled in favor of Barletta. In 1960 Fidel Castro again expropriated him, and Barletta had to go into exile once more. When Trujillo died, Barletta was able to return to the Dominican Republic, where he once again raised capital, until, in 1965, his companies were considerably affected by the civil war in the country. One could say that luck was a partial factor that made his success possible, but when a "miracle" occurs five times, one has to look for its causes in the personal situation of someone who preferred to spend his time productively instead of using it to weep or hate. He channeled all of his creative energy and self-made talent into overcoming every adversity that came his way, and continuing to move forward.[97]

His companies implemented noteworthy journalistic and technological innovations, and he always showed that he had the strategic shrewdness of the great industrial visionaries of his time. Furthermore, it is worth mentioning that the newspaper *El Mundo* was the only one to receive a tribute and official recognition by the Congress of the Republic of Cuba.[98]

It would be unconscionable to deny Amadeo Barletta's human prowess, to conceal his contributions to the national economy and reduce everything to a perverted and fraudulent explanation

---

[97] The journalist Don Bohning, to whom Barletta granted an interview, says that at 74, the entrepreneur was still involved in business. Barletta acknowledged to Bohning that business was his hobby. "For me, Sunday is the worst day of the week because there's nothing to do," he said. Reflecting on the difficulties he had faced in his life, he said with no resentment: "I've had my problems and I've had my successes and I wouldn't change them for anything in the world. They've given me a great deal of satisfaction." (Don Bohning, "He Licks Trouble Every Time", *The Miami Herald*, April 14, 1968, p. 4B)

[98] "The House will today honor during a special session the integrity of El Mundo", *El Mundo*, November 8, 1951.

of his nonexistent mafia association.

5)   The Cuban government's assaults on Amadeo Barletta's reputation occurred at three different times (1960, 1971 and from 1991 to the present day) and were, and are, motivated by campaigns with different objectives.

In 1960, the intention was to justify the auditing of his properties; in particular, the attacks stemmed from the government's eagerness to take over his media empire when the civil war was just starting, which later took on an international tone with the participation of the USSR and the United States. The spurious argument used at the time was that Barletta had benefited from a privileged relationship with Batista, and even with Trujillo.

In 1971, the intention was to discredit the Barletta family—father and son—in order to retaliate against the condemnation, at the urging of Amadeo Barletta, Jr., of the Cuban government by the Inter American Press Association.

After the drug trafficking scandal of 1989, Barletta's person is included in a fantastic plot constructed by a Cuban writer whose work was promoted by the official propaganda machine. This narrative pretends to prove that Cuban history from the early 1930s to 1959 unfolded in response to the control wielded by the Italian-American mafia over the country's economy, politics, and the profits generated by the mafia's criminal activities. There is reason to believe that this third campaign's immediate objective was to lessen the impact of the drug trafficking scandal in the court of national and international opinion, which took place and involved some of the Cuban government's principal leaders and officers.

6) The story of the character assassination of Amadeo Barletta takes on a new relevancy in light of Cuba's current circumstances.

Both in 1991 and again in 2011, the situation in which the Cuban régime finds itself has been very critical. The intensification of its efforts to delegitimize the past is tied to the renewed need to legitimize the present.

However, the government in Havana, which today intends to turn to private enterprise to avert the national economy's bankruptcy and the imminent unemployment of roughly 25% of the workforce, has made no apologies for the prior abuses it committed against small, medium, and large businesses.

National reconstruction is not just an economic challenge, it also includes our historical recollections. What we should be aiming for is a situation in which we work together to reliably establish the facts, even if we later are divided as to the meaning we wish to attribute to them.

Interpretive plurality is not a weakness; rather, it contributes to the articulation of the various options toward which the Cuban people will, in due course, independently and autonomously select their opinions.

Amadeo Barletta's first company was Santo Domingo Motors Company, founded with a bank loan on 12 September 1920. His father-in-law warned him that there were no more than ten possible automobile buyers in Santo Domingo. "He was right. I only sold three cars in the first year," said Amadeo in an interview. Four years later, however, Santo Domingo Motors' earnings were such that they allowed him to open his second company: Dominican Tobacco and Co. It was always Amadeo Barletta's policy to reinvest dividends in the country in which he lived.

Santo Domingo Motors, approaching its tenth anniversary on Presidente Vásquez. 1929

Santo Domingo Motors after the devastation of hurricane San Zenon, 1930

Amadeo Barletta, founder of Santo Domingo Motors Company, is presented with a gilded clock by the Managing Director
of General Motors Overseas D. Corporation, Gregory McNab,
to commemorate the Dominican company's fifty years of service. On the left is Joaquín Balaguer, president of the Dominican Republic, who was present at the anniversary celebrations

The headline mixes a truth with a lie. Barletta was Italian consul during part of Mussolini's time in power, but he never had any relationship whatsoever with the Trujillo régime. They were, in fact, enemies, even before the coup that brought the Dominican dictator to power. From the very start of the revolutionary process of 1959, smear campaigns played a significant role in order to legitimize various types of actions taken against those it considered its adversaries. In the case of businessmen, and even in regards to the market as a wealth-generating mechanism within the economy, these smear campaigns continued until all assets had been entirely expropriated, not just those belonging to tycoons, but to all self-employed workers in 1968.

Refuta Amadeo Barletta las acusaciones que se le hacen

Asegura que no ha sido beneficiario de la dictadura. Exposición sobre sus negocios

El señor Amadeo Barletta nos remite, para su publicación, las declaraciones que seguidamente reproducimos y en las cuales refuta imputaciones que públicamente se le han hecho, con motivo de haber sido dispuesta la confiscación de sus bienes por el Ministerio de Recuperación de Bienes.

Se nos ha comunicado que la nueva dirección del periódico "El Mundo" rehusó dar cabida en sus páginas a las declaraciones del señor Barletta, quien había solicitado allí su publicación.

Las declaraciones del señor Barletta dicen textualmente:

Siendo mi nombre lo único que nadie me puede quitar y lo que con toda seguridad y orgullo puedo legar a mis hijos y nietos, vengo por este medio a negar por las columnas de que he sido objeto por diversos órganos de publicidad.

Sin perjuicio de la acción legal encaminada a disfrazar ante el Ministerio de Recuperación de Bienes Malversados y demás autoridades revolucionarias competentes los extremos que están interesados en investigar, y respecto a los cuales tengo mi conciencia tranquila.

El Ministerio de Recuperación de Bienes ha dispuesto la intervención de algunas empresas, varias de las cuales presido y otras de las que formo parte, sin investigar extremos que se señalan en la Resolución dictada.

El periódico "Revolución" así como otros diarios, han dado informaciones en las que se comentan, como hechos probados, supuestas vinculaciones mías de negocios con la tiranía de Batista.

También en una de esas informaciones se ha señalado el hecho incierto de que yo trataba de cerrar mi negocio en Cuba, cosa completamente falsa.

Supuestas vinculaciones con la tiranía

Lo primero que quiero desvirtuar es la afirmación de que he sido beneficiario de la dictadura. Ninguna de las empresas que presido o integro se ha levantado al amparo del Poder. Para ninguna de ellas he tenido, como era lo usual, en quienes mantenían esos vínculos que a mí atribuyen, financiamientos del BANDES, BANFAIC, FHA, Financiera Nacional ni otro organismo similar del Estado.

No he tenido socios ni he sido socio de ninguno de los personeros de la pasada dictadura en mis negocios. Todas mis empresas han constituido permanentes fuentes de trabajo. Queda, pues, como afirmación absolutamente falsa, mis vínculos con la dictadura.

Contrariamente a esto, en las dos empresas periodísticas en las cuales estoy interesado directamente, como uno de los propietarios o como acreedor y apoderado, tuvieron amplia acogida durante los años del régimen de Batista, destacadas figuras en el campo de la Revolución, las que actuaron con mi asentimiento personal a entera libertad. Esas figuras hoy ocupan pro-

(Finaliza en la pág. 4-B, Col. 3)

Pide Nasser la comunistas de

Atacó en Damasco a los la RAU. Anuncia Kasser

DAMASCO, febrero 23 (AP).— El presidente Nasser atacó duramente dos veces a los comunistas árabes y dijo que los otros países árabes han expulsado tal como lo hizo la República Árabe Unida.

Este fue el ataque más fuerte de Nasser contra "aquellos viles enemigos de la nación árabe" desde que inició su actual gira a Siria, hace 12 días.

Su ataque se produjo en dos discursos consecutivos profun-

Atrapados 106 hombres en una mina de carbón

Ocurrió el accidente en Alemania Oriental

On February 22, 1960 the Cuban press announced the confiscation of the assets of 155 individuals, and a total of 40 companies. It was through the press that Barletta learned his companies were on the list. Two days later he refuted the accusations made against him in the press. His statement was published in the *Diaro de la Marina* because the newspaper *El Mundo*, owned by him but already under the control of people connected to the new government, refused to publish it. Barletta's statement begins as follows: "My name being the only thing no one can take from me and that I can with absolute certainty and pride bequeath to my children and grandchildren, I come to deny through this medium the slander spread about me by various advertising media".

AN ACCOUNT OF HARASSMENT AND DEMONIZATION

Ana Julia Faya

Among other requirements, social science research demands the use of all possible sources, irrespective of their ideologies or politics, if the researcher aspires to be truthful and respectful to their readers or, in the case of a professor, their students. This is why all sources must also be explicitly acknowledged in the finished work or in the lecture given. The point is that evaluating information from all sides contributes to the objectivity that all academicians should instill their findings. Furthermore, such findings should present an assessment of the various, sometimes contradictory hypotheses the scholar has had to peruse during the occasionally arduous and always stressful path of theory creation.

Despite such established norms, the application of these elementary research practices has met with very serious obstacles in Cuba, where official policies and ideological stances weigh on historical, economic, philosophical, or political research, marring the findings of talented scholars who are followers of socialism—or revolutionaries, as the régime's supporters are still called in Cuba—not just those of opponents or dissidents, whose work is rejected out of hand. The number of obstacles increases when an attempt is made to discern the fluctuations in the thinking of one powerful leader—and a totalitarian one at that—and when the likelihood of publication is reduced to what is permitted by the corresponding authorities, be they the Ideological Department of the Central Committee (CC) of the Cuban Communist Party's (CCP), or the academic institution to which one belongs, or the publishing house.

Many social science researchers in Cuba have experienced situations in which they have had to keep their findings quiet, or ended up putting their manuscripts away in a drawer, or have had to write them in such a way that they "say without saying", in a language that is so ambiguous that it almost always alters the message of the article or essay in question. Sometimes they've had to content themselves with merely reading banned books when they have been able to get their hands on them and with discussing their thoughts about them in the sitting rooms of their houses among friends whom they trust completely.

The restrictions and rules imposed on intellectual output are based on the political viewpoints assumed by the leadership. In addition, these rules may correspond mainly to the predominance of specific sectors within the elite, and their interpretation in the institutions where they are applied can be more or less flexible, more or less repressive. They may even lapse into the ridiculous: at academic centers and at the University of Havana, for instance, when writing up the bibliography for scientific works, the sources used were carefully chosen to indicate a balance in favor of those officially recognized, among which the speeches of Fidel Castro or compilations of such speeches had to be given pride of place. The bibliographies of degree and doctoral theses and of the scientific dossiers for obtaining field research positions were headed by the Complete Works of Marx, Engels and Lenin, and by the speeches of Fidel Castro, after which the rest of the literature consulted was listed in alphabetical order as evidence of not only ideological incorruptibility—because this alone is insufficient—but of loyalty to the leader even if the topic of the specialty in question were to be piracy in Caribbean waters or the influence of flamenco on Cuban music.

My experience in academe began inauspiciously in the University of Havana's Philosophy Department, which to a large extent branded my subsequent career. This department, where I studied in order to later become a professor of Marxism, was shut down, and as if to obliterate all traces of it, its publications were destroyed and the building housing it was demolished.

The purpose of the philosophy, the Marxism and the history of Cuban political thinking researched and taught there was to encompass all the creative output in those areas of study, without discriminating against important authors, and to try to avoid the dogmas and manuals in vogue originating from Soviet socialism. In the early 1970s, those of us in the Philosophy Department were accused of being "revisionist" by the Cuban régime's top officials, in particular by the ideological section of the Armed Forces Ministry. Up to that time, we thought we had been interpreting Fidel Castro's thinking and the Marxism we believed upheld it, but we hadn't realized that Castro, after the failure of The Ten Million Ton Sugar Harvest (*La zafra de los diez millones*), had shifted from fostering pockets of guerrillas in Latin America and Africa toward institutionalizing the country in a similar fashion to COMECON member states. The country's ideological orientation and academic output had been taken over by the sectors most closely associated with Soviet policies and by the most dogmatic and simplistic Marxist doctrine.

The literature we used in the Department, which attempted to encompass the thinking of Trotsky, Gramsci, Luxemburg, or Lukács, or to delve into the distinctions between the works of Friedrich Engels relative to those of Karl Marx, or the works of Heidegger or Kierkegaard, the articles in the journal *Pensamiento Crítico* (Critical Thinking), and the research on Cuban thinkers and politicians like Félix Varela, Guiteras, or Chibás, were used against us. Discussions between the two Board of Directors of the Department, *Pensamiento Crítico*, and a Party commission chaired by President Osvaldo Dorticós were unsuccessful. Most of the department's rank and file, even those of us who were never able to publish our work or teach a class, were brought before a tribunal composed of the university's CCP leaders and professors who saw to it that we were separated from each other and reassigned to faculties within the University or to other institutions in the country. This was after subjecting us to an interrogation on what they considered to be the "principles" that should be guiding us, followed by a strong reprimand if our answers were not to their liking. As of that moment, I became one of the "Philosophy revisionists", a kind of tropical pariah to whom it was inadvisable to get too close if you wanted to survive in that society.

At the time, the individuals making up the elite under the Cuban totalitarian régime did not constitute a monolith. Within that elite there still coexisted representatives from the various political streams who were part of the insurrection against Fulgencio Batista's dictatorship: communists from the Popular Socialist Party, anticommunists, dogmatics, antidogmatics, Fidelistas, Guevaristas, pro-Soviets and others not so much, all living under actually existing socialism. These different attitudes and visions regarding Fidel Castro's Cuba allowed me, despite the Philosophy Department baggage I carried, to work at the State Council's Publications Office (*Oficina de Publicaciones del Consejo de Estado*, OPCE) on Revolution Plaza under the supervision of Celia Sánchez.

Even there, however inherent to the régime, I also witnessed censuring and prohibitions and the fabrication of images regarding the course of the country and its leaders. For instance, one of my assignments was to prepare a photo-illustrated chronology, from 1959 to 1975, entitled *Dieciséis años de Revolución* (Sixteen Years of Revolution) to be published at the time the First Party Congress would be held. For several months a historian and I worked together at newspaper and magazine archives as well as at the National Library after a letter signed by Celia Sánchez gave us complete access to archives of public sources from the 1960s, which by that point had been made unavailable to the public. When choosing photos in which Fidel Castro was featured, one of the requirements was that he could not appear wearing glasses or be caught with sardonic facial expressions, but rather valiant or pleasant ones.

We finished the chronography and Celia called a meeting to present it for critical review.

Representatives from Raúl Castro's office objected to almost 40 percent of the photographs. First in line was the historic photo of January 2, 1959, showing Fidel Castro calling for a general strike while surrounded by a group of Rebel Army members, including Carlos Franqui, who had recently gone into exile. We were given a replacement photo with Franqui's image deleted, a technique similar to that used by Stalinism in the USSR. Another objection was concerned with the 1965 exodus of Cubans to the United States via the port of Camarioca, the idea being that no importance would be given to those leaving the country. However, the main objections pertained to the number of times then President Osvaldo Dorticós appeared compared to Raúl Castro. We were even given a percentage for photos of Fidel, another for those of Raúl, and the then president was left with a minimal percentage of photos. The significance of the events being illustrated, whether national or international, did not matter, events which by their very nature—such as the welcome given to Indonesia's President Sukarno in Havana—required the presence of the nation's President, not that of the Commander in Chief of the Armed Forces. The chronography was never published.

Another one of my assignments at the OPCE was an inquiry into the April 1958 General Strike, soon after the overseas publication of a book by Carlos Franqui for which the author had used documents and films from the Council of State's Office of Historical Affairs (*Oficina de Asuntos Históricos*). Apparently, the intention was to present an official version of the facts that the exiled Franqui had documented with facsimiles. I was given complete access to Fidel Castro's historical archives and to his Office of Shorthand Versions (*Oficina de Versiones Taquigráficas*). I also conducted interviews with over 200 of the strike participants from provinces all over the country, including lengthy sessions with individuals sentenced for political reasons and about to be released, like David Salvador, and with national leaders of the 26th of July Movement (M26-7) like Faustino Pérez.

After two years' work, the end-result, numbering over 200 pages, was not published. My conclusions did not highlight the persona of Fidel Castro, nor the heroism of the Sierra rebels, who barely carried out military actions in April 1958, but rather the activities of a very dynamic civil society in the early months of that year under Batista (which could not be compared with the faltering reality of the 1970's). In addition, the work underscored the actions, organization and coordination of the M26-7 leadership, packed with personalities with dissimilar ideological tendencies—and also with flaws since one outcome was the failure of the strike—in whose hands lay the Movement's real power up to the time of the April Strike. The work also narrated the heated arguments between PSP (Popular Socialist Party) communists and M26-7 leaders; and it described, as a watershed in the story, the meeting at Mompié where, with a serious debacle on their shoulders, the *Llano* leaders were made to buckle under the Sierra leaders[99], while Che acted as prosecutor and the rebels kept their rifles at the ready.

The demonization of those of us who belonged to the Philosophy Department resurfaced in my case when in 1980 I decided to work at the Center for European Studies (*Centro de Estudios Europeos*, CEE) attached to the CC of the CCP. Almost ten years had gone by since the Department's prior episode, during which time I heard of several cases of harassment and discrimination against former colleagues. Some were unable to obtain another academic post; another was harassed by party authorities until he resigned from

---

[99] The power struggle between Fidel and the formal governing body of M26-7 came to be known as the *Sierra* versus the *Llano*, or cities. It pitted Fidel and his group of guerrillas against the movement's formal leadership based in the major cities. After the failure of the April Strike, and the military offensive that followed, Fidel and his rebels took over the leadership of the M26-7.

his post as professor of Cuban history at the University, accused of having used his class to emphasize the devastation caused by the tactic of torching cane plantations, a tactic used by Máximo Gómez during the War of Independence, and also for refusing to find Marxism in the works of José Martí; another group decided to form a band was able to obtain permits to travel abroad on artistic tours, but only after heated arguments with leaders of the Young Communists Union, who were refusing them the permits for ideological reasons; still others were the object of fabricated accusations, which they expiated in detentions at the hands of the State Security apparatus.

Given these realities, when I was informed that my request to join the CEE was denied with no further explanation, I decided to investigate, and I discovered that CCP members within the CEE had vetoed me because a researcher who had belonged to the Philosophy Department was already working at the Center and they did not want to run the "ideological risk" of our being together. I therefore filed a formal complaint with party authorities, leveraging the privileged status afforded by my closeness to Celia Sánchez. In the complaint letter, I held that I did not accept the arguments against me unless hard evidence was provided of my "ideological problems". I explained my situation to Celia in a letter and met with her for over an hour — a meeting that was illuminating in regards to the characteristics of the groups and individuals within the elite, including Fidel Castro—as a result of which the Central Committee's Office of Appeals and Sanctions (*Oficina de Apelaciones y Sanciones*, OAS) took over the case.

After Celia Sánchez's death, and unwilling to join a hostile community at the CEE, I began to work as an officer of the Americas Department at the CC of the CCP, headed by Manuel Piñeiro, a personal friend and collaborator of Celia's. Here, the access I had to classified information enabled me to learn of the destructive opinions about me expressed by CC officials during the investigation undertaken by the OAS, even though these individuals neither knew me personally nor had worked with me; as far as they were concerned, the mere knowledge that I had belonged to the Philosophy Department was enough to condemn me.

After several months, as a result of the OAS's inquiries and the parallel complaints submitted to the country's authorities by former Philosophy Department colleagues, a Commission was set up composed of Central Committee members. They heard several of our cases and issued a document to clarify that our having been part of the staff of that Department did not constitute grounds for any kind of discrimination, although the ambiguous language in which it was written did not make it clear if we were absolved of all blame. Many of us accepted it as a "Letter of Marque" that we were willing to live with, but it did not prevent our continuing dilemma of being viewed as intellectuals who needed to be closely watched.

This special "surveillance", and many other significant situations that emerged at the Center, led to the dismantling, in 1966, of the Center for American Studies (*Centro de Estudios sobre América*, CEA), where at various times six former colleagues from the old Philosophy Department had joined the CEA staff as researchers, including me. Charges of "fifth columnists" and "agents of imperialism" read by Raúl Castro in the Report before the Fifth Plenary Session of the Central Committee initiated one of the most ignominious instances of intellectual repression of the 1990s in Cuba. The Second Secretary of the CCP once again aimed his attacks against the Philosophy Department and the whole of the CEA: "In the past twenty-five years, I've batted two long drives against the group," he said in a memo dated May 24, 1996 (Maurizio Giuliano, 1998).

I am absolved of the retelling of this process, its national and international repercussions, and the fate of most of us by Giuliano's terrific and above-quoted book, *The CEA Case. Intellectuals, Inquisitors - Perestroika on the Island?* (*El caso CEA. Intelectuales, Inquisidores, ¿Perestroika en la Isla?*), a detailed and well-documented analysis of this scandal of intellectual repression of which we were victims at the hands of the upper echelons of Cuba's leadership, several of us twice over. In writing the book, Giuliano used (and reproduced) the records of the discussions between the CEA's Board of Directors and the Commission set up by the Politburo of the CCP, those of the CCP nucleus within the CEA, interviews with several researchers, and public information available in Cuba and other countries during the months of March through October 1996, which practically turns the book into a primary source.

Suffice it to say that the experiences in the Philosophy Department in the early 1970's, the personal experience of many of us in subsequent years, together with the new political circumstances of 1990's Cuba and the singularity that all those of us who were accused were members of the CCP, enabled us to act collectively—and unanimously—in regards to the charges leveled against us by the Party itself. However, we also saw for ourselves that our demands that we be cleared of the charges made known all over the country with the publication in *Granma* of the *Report to the Fifth Plenary Session* and with the summons to a discussion of the Report in the workplace and in the Committees for the Defense of the Revolution, were not addressed. The charges stood and the Center was dismantled.

The CEA researchers' "sin", as had previously been the case in the Philosophy Department, consisted of carrying out the most honest academic practice according to our ideological convictions at the time, even when the findings of our research differed from official policies. This, however, is not recognized under totalitarian régimes, where the political and propaganda machines impose the rules of the game and one pays dearly when the decisions regarding what may be researched, said, and published about certain topics, facts, and individuals are not followed to the letter.

In the photo on the left, taken at the moment Fidel Castro is calling for a general strike in January 1959, Carlos Franqui appears in the center. Subsequently, when Franqui went into exile, the Cuban government tampered with the photograph to erase his image, as can be seen in the photo on the right.

THE HOW AND WHY OF THE ATTEMPTED ASSASSINATION OF MY REPUTATION

Carlos Alberto Montaner

Although what follows is a description of my own experience as a case study, before I commence it seems pertinent to first detail certain aspects of my experience as a victim of a constant and steadfast smear campaign. The slander and insults of which I have been and continue to be the target are not an isolated or atypical phenomenon. On the contrary, they are part of a general repressive strategy that lies at the heart of totalitarian dictatorships.

Political Legitimacy and Official History

What is the reason behind this brutal discrediting of democratic opponents? A fundamental one: the political legitimacy of the Cuban dictatorship is based on the purported infinite wisdom of its leader, a warlord who always speaks ex cathedra. There is no room for dissension or doubt. As was the case with academic teachings in the Middle Ages, all truths have already been expressed or uncovered by the authorities. To think otherwise, to entertain a different point of view, turns the individual who expresses that disagreement, doubt, or independent thought into a heretic who must be punished or excised from society.

In Cuba's case, there are not even authorities in the plural sense. There is only one: the authority is and has been Fidel Castro, whose word and whose speeches constitute the sect's sacred texts. It is of no consequence that Castro has contradicted himself countless times. Each rectification is an expression of the truth, and does not have to be put to the test, explained, nor the altered opinion justified. His supporters and the general population are not there to think for themselves, but to obey and applaud. Above all, to be a *revolutionary* in Castro's Cuba is to renounce the power of personally judging reality. That is the leader's task.

The official history is very simple: Fidel Castro, his brother Raúl, and their revolutionary comrades are the heirs to the nationalist, anti-imperialist and anti-American 19th-century *mambís*. They picked up the torch dropped by Martí after his death in 1895 (a legacy betrayed by the politicians of the pseudo republic founded in 1902) for the purpose of creating a just and educated society, equipped with an extensive sanitation system, far removed from exploitation by foreign capitalists and their lackeys, the Cuban capitalists. This revolution, obviously, had to take place within Marxist-Leninist parameters because this was the political ideology of speedy progress and development.

Aside from this capricious narrative, completely at odds with historical reality, and the fact that this peculiar ideological option was failing in twenty countries, it was vital to believe that Fidel Castro, Raúl, and their principal supporters, aides, and accomplices possessed the essential virtues of principled and incorruptible individuals. It had to be taken for granted that they were all honest, selfless, austere, hard-working, faithful to the truth, and willing to give their lives for the ideal of turning Cuba into a happy and prosperous country of citizens proud to have constituted a nation guided by ethics, and devoted to the salvation of less fortunate peoples.

To be a revolutionary is to believe in exactly that. Conversely, to be a counterrevolutionary is to question it.

Naturally, the real Cuba was far removed from this absurd historical and moral simplification that was so unlike reality. The truth was that on that poor island, the implementation of a communist dictatorship had brought with it as many setbacks as in other countries that at some time have experimented with that calamitous system.

The reality was that the revolutionary political discourse, based on a falsification of history, was unsustainable when compared to the obvious fact that the power structure, beginning with the Castro brothers, was as clumsy, corrupt, and negligent as that of any communist tyranny after half a century in power. The unproductiveness and physical quasi-demolition of the country left no room for doubt.

Despite the observable evidence, it was relatively easy to impose uniformity within Cuba and turn the whole of society into an immense chorus of sycophants dedicated to singing the praises of the régime. In a relatively short period of time, the entire power structure and all officials with access to the media learned what it was they had to do and say in order to remain in their posts: achieved through rewards and punishments—many more punishments than rewards.

Furthermore, from the beginnings of the revolution guidelines were already being firmly set in place for repressive measures to be adopted to punish those who dared dissent. From the moment Commander Huber Matos was declared a traitor and sentenced to twenty years in prison for having written a simple resignation letter to Fidel Castro, everyone knew what to expect. The best way to survive was to play pretend.

Defamation as a political weapon

Naturally, the dictatorship faced a serious problem with Cubans who criticized the revolution. Since the issue was one of a régime based on an indisputable dogma—Fidel's infallibility, the certainty of his official truth and his irreproachable ethical nature—it was unthinkable that these opponents could be right, or even partly so, which meant they had to be countered, but not by debating their arguments, since this would mean entering dangerous territory where the government could lose, but by trying to destroy the reputation of these inconvenient and rebellious Cubans.

In order to silence them, Cuban oppositionists were constantly accused of being one, some, or all of the following:

- Batista-supporters wanting to return to the era of the corrupt dictatorship that was toppled by the revolution;

- torturers belonging to the Batista tyranny;

- oligarchs who were resentful because they had been deprived of their assets;

- ambitious individuals holding a grudge against the Revolution because they had fought against Batista only to pursue some important post in the future revolutionary government, only to find such posts were unattainable;

- fascists who detested the prominent role of the masses;

- racists upset at the egalitarian measures dictated by the revolution favoring blacks;

- CIA agents;

- terrorists;

- amoral individuals bought by Washington's gold or that of large financial corporations;

- riff raff invariably motivated by shameful interests;

- the cruel enemies of a decent people who were fighting tooth and nail to make progress while being persecuted by U.S. imperialism.

One adjective, also used by Hitler to refer to the Jews, summarized the caricature of opponents of the communist dictatorship: they were *gusanos* or worms. They were disgusting animals who did not deserve to live and who could be trampled underfoot with no moral compunction.

However, this brutal way of discrediting adversaries was not a visceral reaction inspired in a moment of rage. On the contrary, it was a methodical plan aimed at accomplishing three objectives leading to the consolidation of totalitarian power:

1. Confirm the greatness of the revolution and its leaders by comparing them to their despicable enemies.

2. Silence the opposition's arguments by demonizing those who criticize the Cuban government, blocking their access to the media.

3. Dissuade any Cuban from expressing a critical position, given the extremely high price he or she would have to pay.

How does the Cuban government orchestrate its character assassination campaigns? Most likely by following very closely the eleven recommendations or *principles* some have attributed to Goebbels, the Nazi genius behind this form of dirty propaganda:

The principle of simplification and of only one enemy. Adopt a single idea, a single symbol. Individualize the adversary into a single enemy.

The transmission method principle. Merge various adversaries into one category or individual. Adversaries must constitute a single sum total.

The transposition principle. Attribute to the adversary one's own mistakes or faults, answering attack with attack. "If you can't deny bad news, invent others that will distract."

The exaggeration and misrepresentation principle. Turn any anecdote, however small, into a serious threat.

The popularization principle. All propaganda must be popularized, tailoring its level to the least intelligent of those individuals at whom it is targeted. The larger the masses to be convinced, the smaller the mental effort that must be made to understand the message. The receptive capacity of the masses is limited and their understanding is generally poor; in addition, they forget very easily.

The orchestra principle. Propaganda must be limited to a small number of ideas that must be persistently repeated, presenting them over and over again from various perspectives, but always converging on the same concept. Unwaveringly and without hesitation. This is where the famous phrase comes from: "If a lie is repeated often enough, it ends up becoming the truth".

The renewal principle. New information and arguments must be constantly issued at such a rate that when the adversary reacts, the public interest will already be focused on something else. The adversary's responses must never be able to counteract the increasing level of accusations against them.

The plausibility principle. Build arguments based on various sources, either via so-called trial balloons or with incomplete information.

The silencing principle. Hush up issues for which a case cannot be made and conceal news items favoring the adversary, in addition to using counterprogramming with the help of the associated media.

The transfusion principle. As a rule of thumb, propaganda always builds on a preexisting substratum, be it a national mythology or a system of traditional hates and prejudices. The idea is to disseminate arguments that can grab ahold of primitive attitudes.

The unanimity principle. Convince a great many people that they think "like everyone else," thus creating a false sense of unity.

My Case

We come finally to "my case". For many years now the Cuban intelligence services have been periodically attacking my image. These attacks, filled with shameful lies, are sometimes published in the newspaper Granma and then are reproduced in various Latin American or Internet media outlets that are controlled or infiltrated by the dictatorship's political police. Sometimes the reverse happens: the attacks begin in a media outlet outside Cuba and Granma then picks them up.

Frequently, when I give a conference or present books in Latin America, Spain, and even in Italy, the Cuban embassy, through its sympathizers, organizes condemnatory actions in an attempt to shut me up and intimidate my hosts. In Argentina (as well as in Buenos Aires and Rosario) they even set vehicle tires on fire, while outside the venue they insulted and mistreated those attending my talks. In Colombia, according to what I was told by the Colombian authorities, a network of Internet surfers controlled from Caracas by Cuban services, and headed by a gentleman named Alfredo García, carried out a lengthy campaign designed to remove me from the media outlets that reproduced my columns.

At least twice now, leaflets criticizing me have been published and distributed, and at least once they have gone to the extreme of sending me a bomb inside a book entitled *Una muerte muy dulce* (A Very Easy Death). The package was sent to my office in Madrid and the aim was not to kill me, but to intimidate me so I would stop speaking and writing publicly. It was not rigged to explode.

The defamations that are incessantly repeated against me insist that:

- *My father was a torturer and a Batista supporter.* In fact, my father was Fidel Castro's friend and a fellow member of the Orthodox Party. When Fidel was imprisoned in Isla de Pinos, my father, a well-known journalist, publicly fought for his freedom, which Fidel was grateful for as evidenced in Fidel's correspondence with Luis Conte Agüero. My father, by the way, was not the only family member who was a friend of Fidel Castro's: so was my father's first cousin, José de Jesús Ginjauma Montaner (Pepe Jesús), Fidel Castro's former boss in the *Unión Insurreccional Revolucionaria* (UIR or Revolutionary Insurrectionist Union). Due to these links with my family, Fidel used to visit our home on Tejadillo Street in Old Havana in the late forties and early fifties.

- *I am an agent of the CIA,* initially posted by their agency in Puerto Rico and then in Spain, a charge that is absolutely false and made without the slightest proof or the slightest documented support, even though the Cuban services agency has requested (and obtained) my dossier from the federal government under the Freedom of Information Act. I lived in Puerto Rico while teaching literature at a university and then moved to Spain for my doctorate. In Spain, where I have lived for four decades, I founded a small publishing company devoted to publishing books about learning the Spanish language. While the firm existed, we also published over 500 books on language and literature. Since I have never ceased to be an exiled democrat, we published a few Cuban studies that demonstrated the dictatorship's cruelty towards homosexuals, and highlighted their other human rights violations. Furthermore, since the early seventies, U.S. legislation has prohibited its government agents from working in U.S. media outlets that disseminate information within the United States. I have worked for *The Miami Herald* for several decades and I presently work for CNN, to mention just two of the U.S. media outlets to which I have been or am connected. None of this would have been possible were it true that I am a CIA agent.

- *I am a terrorist* because fifty years ago, when I was 17 years old, I was detained with three other students (one of them, Alfredo Carrión Obeso, was murdered in prison by the guards) and sentenced to prison for political crimes. This also is not true. During the trial we were not charged with any specific act of terrorism because, in fact, we had not committed any. Had we done so, in those days, (early 1961), I do not have the slightest doubt that we would have been shot, as was the fate of many young men during that period of constant executions by firing squad. In reality, terrorism is revolting to me. Just as under Batista's dictatorship I thought it despicable for the 26th of July Movement to plant bombs designed to kill or mutilate innocent people, as indeed happened on more than one occasion, or that it hijack airplanes, as they did with a Cubana de Aviación aircraft in late 1958, an episode during which several completely innocent children and adults lost their lives. I have never been of the mind that "the end justifies the means". That vile way of thinking belongs to the Cuban dictatorship, not to me.

- *I was trained as a U.S. army officer at Fort Benning.* I have never set foot in the place. I have never been an officer of the United States Army and the military has never been remotely close to becoming my vocation. On the other hand, I did enlist as a soldier in the "Unidades Cubanas" (Cuban Units), as they were then called, during the October 1962 Missile Crisis—first, we were sent to Fort Knox and from there we were transferred to Fort Jackson—in the belief that we had to fight against Soviet interference in Cuba. After the agreement between Kennedy and Khrushchev was settled, the missiles were removed from Cuba and we recruits were stuck in the U.S. army for six useless months until we were able to get discharged. I, and several young men who had undergone this experience then tried to create an organization capable of fighting in order to regain freedom for Cubans, but we failed before we even began and within a few months, the group was quietly dissolved.

To spread these lies, the Cuban government uses different mouthpieces and officials, but the person who has been assigned the task of regularly attacking me is a Canadian journalist and refugee in Cuba with links to the Ministry of the Interior named Jean-Guy Allard, who remains unforgiven by his countrymen for one of his primary roles, which was to prepare intelligence reports on Canadian officials in contact with Cuba, an activity that falls under the category of treason in his country of origin.

Why have the defamatory attacks against me intensified? Most likely in order to silence me, but especially because some twenty years ago, while living in Madrid in the 1990's, I contributed decisively to the creation of the *Plataforma Democrática Cubana* (Cuban Democratic Platform), a coalition of liberals, Christian-democrats, and social democrats that sought to bring about a peaceful transition away from the régime, similar to what the Spaniards experienced after Franco's death, and with touch points on par with the initiatives being undertaken at the time by Europeans in the ex-Soviet satellites to inaugurate their new-found freedom after the fall of the Berlin Wall.

For the Cuban dictatorship, the notion of this coalition was an object of fierce condemnation. It was deemed more dangerous that a direct threat of violence and, as a result, they gave themselves over to the task of presenting our proposal of opening a dialogue as if it were a sinister initiative by the CIA and not what it truly was: A totally independent attempt to remove the conflict of Cuba from the cockfight between Washington and Havana and put it in its proper place: a civilized confrontation between Cuban democrats, (backed by democrats the world over), and the last Stalinist dictatorship in the Western world.

From that point on, the régime's defamation apparatus, coordinated by the *Departamento de Orientación Revolucionaria* (Department of Revolutionary Orientation), the notorious DOR, intensified its campaign— translating it, in addition, into several languages because it understood the threat to be international.

The Internet and Wikipedia

In order to achieve its objectives, the Cuban dictatorship has ironically been helped by one of its most dangerous enemies: the Internet. The government uses the same instrument that it fears like the devil—and which it has obsessively dedicated itself to controlling, so as to prevent citizens from being informed and informing others—to spread and multiply its lies, using numerous cyber-warriors affiliated with the Ministry of the Interior, and students at the Computer Science University who are expert opinion-makers via virtual networks.

Amidst this constant battle, one website is of particular importance to the Cuban dictatorship: Wikipedia, a virtual, free content encyclopedia used by the majority of the world's students and media, where the Cuban government can write and rewrite however it pleases the biographies of its friends and enemies, with the added advantage that it appears to be an independent medium.

Given my personal experience with Wikipedia, I will take the liberty of referencing what I at one point wrote in one of my columns:

The Wikipedia Battle

In the mid-18th century, a Parisian editor asked the writer Denis Diderot to create a work that would contain all relevant knowledge of the time. Thus, over the course of 26 years there emerged the 28 volumes of the French Encyclopedia, written by the most esteemed (and courageous) intellectuals of the era—some 160 authors including Voltaire, Rousseau and Montesquieu. The books included over 60,000 articles and almost 3,000 illustrations. A few years after their publication, the French Revolution broke out and the *ancien régime* was annihilated. Although it is impossible to prove, there is undoubtedly a link between these two events. It was not long before the guillotine began coming down.

The encyclopedia of our time is called Wikipedia. It is an anonymous, collective work edited on the Internet, to which an army of volunteers contributes spontaneously and without guidance. Its dimensions and impact are infinitely greater than that of the collection edited by Diderot. A few days ago, Carmen Pérez-Lanzac summarized this editorial phenomenon in [the newspaper] *El País*: in its just over eight years of existence, it has already collected 11 million articles prepared by 150,000 authors in 265 languages, although English, naturally, is the dominant one. In Spanish articles alone, there are already 482,000 entries to which some 400 are added every day.

Is this enormous mass of information reliable? Only relatively so, as the experts incessantly warn, but according to Google's implacable accounting, it is the most viewed and used source of information. By whom? By students, who need to write their papers; by journalists, overwhelmed by the lack of time; by anyone who urgently needs a piece of information and generally finds nothing closer at hand than the information contained in Wikipedia.

This is a very dangerous issue because Wikipedia is also an ideological battleground where there is no shortage of lies or biased selection of information to distort the image of adversaries that one or many wish to destroy. Wikipedia has a large number of contributors devoted to the healthy dissemination of knowledge, but there are also many warriors who have resolved to destroy the reputation of those whom they consider to be their enemies.

I learned of all this first-hand when a former student of mine warned me that my biography on Wikipedia described me as a terrorist at the service of the CIA who had assassinated priests and perpetrated who knows how many other far-fetched fantasies. Since I am not at all technically savvy, I asked him to get in touch with the organizers of Wikipedia and explain the slander of which I was the object. They listened to him, investigated the facts and allegations, deleted the most obvious falsehoods and placed a "lock" on the page so that the slanderers would be unable to rewrite their vile lies.

While amending this Wikipedia page, my former student found out that one of the sources of disinformation was the Computer Science University in Havana, constructed over what used to be the Lourdes espionage base that was created by the Soviets in Cuba during the Cold War, where "digital action commandos" have been appointed to write and rewrite the biographies of friends and enemies according to the script dictated by the political police. For them, Wikipedia is a battleground on which they forge the image of reality that serves the interests of the revolution. Never before, they claim, have they had such a formidable, free, anonymous (thus freeing them from criminal liability) and effective propaganda machine at their disposal. I can easily imagine that they must also fantasize about putting the guillotine back to work.

The End of This Story

Nevertheless, all of these attempts to vilify their adversaries and shape a version of history and reality tailored to the revolution's discourse will ultimately prove to be completely useless. The USSR, which was the Cuban government's instructor in these matters, also openly and without any trace of decency disparaged its opponents, but whether their tactics were aiming for a medium- or long-term effect, all of it was in vain. While the pawns of power during the Communist dictatorship are today detested or ignored by the Russian people, the prestige and reputation of men like Sakharov and Solzhenitsyn have been completely restored. Character assassination is never conclusive. The same will happen in Cuba.

If you do a Google search with the words "Carlos Alberto Montaner CIA", the first reference that appears is the newspaper *Granma*, the official publication of the Cuban Communist Party. April 30, 2011

The accusations against Carlos Alberto Montaner circulated by the Cuban government and its allies on the Internet are innumerable, varied and continuous.

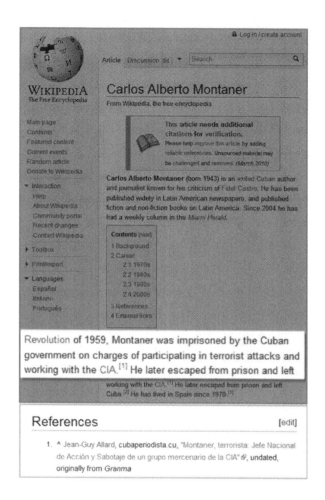

working with the CIA.[1] He later escaped from prison and left
Cuba.[2] He has lived in Spain since 1970.[3]

References [edit]

1. ^ Jean-Guy Allard, cubaperiodista.cu, "Montaner, terrorista: Jefe Nacional
de Acción y Sabotaje de un grupo mercenario de la CIA" ☞, undated,
originally from *Granma*

One website is particularly important to the Cuban government: Wikipedia, a virtual, free content encyclopedia read by most of the world's students and media, where Cuban officials can write and rewrite with complete freedom the biographies of their friends and enemies.

The principal source for the attacks against Carlos Alberto Montaner are signed by Canadian journalist Jean-Guy Allard, a refugee in Cuba.

The photo on the left is from the blog *El Republicano Liberal* (The Liberal Republican). The one on the right is the same photo, edited to add the CIA's logo in the background and posted in the blog *Cambios en Cuba* (Changes in Cuba) by Manuel Henríquez Lagarde along with a reproduction of an article by Jean-Guy Allard.

In the blog *Cambios en Cuba*, Henríquez Lagarde also posts hostile articles against the blogger Yoani Sánchez and the independent press in Cuba.

READY, AIM, FIRE... IN ITALY

Gordiano Lupi

Italian Surveillance Committees

Journalists shouldn't talk about personal situations. I'm making an exception because what happened to my wife can serve as firsthand proof of the ambiguity prevailing in the Cuban political system. The premise of a non-democratic Cuba, particularly one that is so far removed from the most basic principles of rule of law, is easy to prove, but there are those in Italy will that not yield to evidence. As a Cuban friend of mine says, all of Castro's defenders live abroad so they do not have to put up with the humiliations of a perverse political system. Punishments for sustaining certain political beliefs are one of them.

So let's get to the facts: On August 25, 2006, a sudden ring of the telephone shattered the peace and quiet of a summer afternoon in Tuscany. My wife answered. On the line, a female voice with a strong Caribbean accent (a Cuban embassy employee) asked her for personal information and called her "comrade", which was unusual jargon there.

"We have received an urgent notice from the Immigration Office in Havana.[100] You have thirty days to report to our offices where you will be given precise information regarding the message, after which you must immediately leave for Cuba."

"What do you mean?" my wife asked with concern. "Has something serious happened?"

"Your foreign residence permit has been revoked."

"After living in Italy for eight years? I don't understand."

"I can't tell you anything more over the phone. You must come to the embassy."

"I'm pregnant. I can't take such a long trip and I can't travel to Havana in this condition. If you can't tell me anything over the phone, then write to me."

"All I can tell you is that according to the message, you are considered a person who is politically active against the Cuban government. If you do not appear in person, you will automatically lose your foreign resi-

---

[100] Dirección de Inmigración y Extranjería del Ministerio del Interior [Editor's Note]

dence permit and be classified as a person who has definitively exited the country" [101]

For those of you personally unfamiliar with the peculiarities of a dictatorship that grants virtually no rights to its citizens, you should know that to be classified under the status of "definitive exit" is the worst thing that can happen to a Cuban living abroad. Such person is considered from then on a *gusano* (worm), an antisocial individual, a counterrevolutionary. Such persons are not entitled to enter Cuba even if they have a valid Cuban or foreign passport. If they wish to visit the Island they must request a special permit from the embassy. If the permit is granted, they may return to visit family members, but there are well-founded fears that once there they may not be allowed to leave the country.

"Deep down I already felt like an emigrant and had decided not to return to Cuba. What I regret is that you are imposing this condition on me. In any case, I will not go to your offices. Do whatever you deem appropriate. Fortunately, I'm an Italian citizen." End of conversation.

---

[101] "Salida definitiva del pais" is a category that implies that the person will never again be allowed to live in Cuba and from then on can only visit the Island as a tourist for a period of one month at a time. [Editor's Note]

I decided to share this personal anecdote for those of you that may still harbor illusions as to the virtuousness of Cuba's "real existing socialism". One major achievement of that "socialism" has been to rip away basic political and civil rights such as the right to freedom of movement.

My wife has never publicly expressed opinions against the régime; she has never written an article nor given interviews about the Cuban situation. She has never been a political activist. The bottom line is that she has "to pay" for my articles, my books and for the novels of her cousin, Alejandro Torreguitart Ruiz.

Politically incorrect expressions are monitored by the Cuban embassies with the friendly assistance of Italians allied with the Cuban government. That group of loyal, true believers not only presents Italians with an ideal vision of the reality within the island but also monitors and vehemently slanders the "enemy" fellow Italians in our own country.

The "other wall" for character assassination is installed in Italy with local "gunners". The most remarkable among them is, undoubtedly, Gianni Minà.

The Italian Magazine, *Latinoamerica,* and the Cuban Régime

Latinoamerica[102], a magazine edited by Gianni Minà[103] publishes articles about all the southern parts of the world. It is one of the few publications where one can read about Nicaragua, about Honduras, or the Zapatistas all in one place. The issue I take with it in particular are the articles dealing with Cuba. Perhaps it's because I know Cuba well, but when I see an article by Gianni Minà's saying that the Pope's position on Cuba is further to the left than that of the *Diesse*[104], it makes me laugh. You have to ask yourself what anyone could mean by "a left-wing discourse" on Cuba in the present day. Certainly the U.S. embargo is unfair—no one denies this. But we can also say that the embargo does Fidel Castro a favor because he uses it as an excuse to justify all the accumulated failures throughout the half century in which he has exercised absolute power. In my opinion, being on the left and talking about Cuba today means being on the side of the Cuban people, not on the side of the dictator.

---

[102] Official site: **http://www.giannimina-latinoamerica.it/**

[103] Born 1938. Award-winning Italian journalist, writer, and television host. [Editor's Note]

[104] DS: Italy's left-wing party. [Editor's Note]

Another problematic article about Cuba was authored by WuMing4[105]. Some of what he says is fair, but other topics he avoids. The article seems to have been written by a special visiting guest of the government, who saw only what the régime wanted to show him. He writes of police officers who lovingly look after tourists and watch over their safety. True. They do that, too. But their main duty is to make life impossible for Cubans trying to *resolver*[106]. They confiscate goods that are sold in the black market, arrest those who strive to find a way to feed their children, prevent anyone from doing anything that would not constitute as a crime anywhere except, perhaps, in North Korea.

WuMing4 describes a protest march along *El Malecón*[107] against European sanctions as a gathering of conscientious and indignant Cubans marching in a spontaneous demonstration. False. It is, as usual, the

---

[105] Federico Guglielmi (Wu Ming 4). Wu Ming is a pseudonym for a group of Italian authors formed in 2000. Wu Ming's members are typically known as Wu Ming 1, 2, 3, 4 and 5.

[106] A popular Cuban expression that translates as: trying to find the basic means for survival, whether it involves buying simple products or finding necessary services, either which must almost always be "resolved" via the black market or else by claiming personal favors. [Editor's Note]

[107] The seawall stretching for 8 km along Havana's coast. [Editor's Note]

régime that organizes buses to pick up forced volunteers from their jobs and schools, who are then directed to recite, under a blazing sun, slogans conceived by the ideological machinery of the Party. Much like when the so-called "elections" for the People's Power (with only one official candidate on the slate) are held. On these occasions they come to your home to get you out to vote "yes". No wonder the "spontaneous enthusiasm" for participating in such "elections" is always reported to be high.

WuMing4 compares the state of information in Italy with that of Cuba. This, too, is false. In Cuba, the only access to information consists of the pages printed by the régime (and reproduced, in various forms, by its propaganda machinery), which WuMing4 must have read if he indeed was there on a special visit. In his article, WuMing4 goes to the extreme of saying that the prison for *jineteras*[108] is called Villa Delicia and that it's not particularly harsh, but a place where these women make themselves useful by providing social services. One can tell that he has never spoken with a *jinetera* who has been in that prison; he would otherwise be aware of what conditions there are really like. There are many testimonies from journalists and visitors to

---

[108] Cuban slang for female hookers, especially those who target foreign tourists. [Editor's Note]

Cuba that belied that sugar-coated version of the repression and imprisonment of prostitutes. In a book I plan to publish sometime soon (*Vedere Cuba Dalla Parte Dei Cubani* or *Mirar a Cuba con la piel de un Cubano*), I step into the shoes of those Cubans who have to live on a few dollars a month in a society where it is hard to gain them. Poverty is one of the main causes of prostitution anywhere, but Castro's devotees in foreign countries choose not to look into that aspect of the problem.

Granma, the Official Cuban Paper, is Now Available in Italian!

On October 2007, an Italian printed edition of *Granma*, the official newspaper of the Cuban Communist Party, and the target of sour jokes in the Island began to circulate once a month, along with with *La Rinascita della sinistra* as a gift from Oliviero Diliberto[109]. We are heading in the wrong direction if the "rebirth of the left" requires organizing propaganda for a dictator.

The journalist Maurizio Musolino[110] understood that the paper of the Cuban communists was not

---

[109] Born 1966. Italian politician. Oliviero Diliberto is the current leader of the Party of Italian Communists. [Editor's Note]

[110] Born 1964. Italian journalist, writer, and communist politician. [Editor's Note]

known for being a paragon of objectivity. He specified that the Italian *Granma* would talk about the changes in Cuba without propaganda, but let's be realistic: if you eliminate the propaganda from *Granma*, there would be nothing left. *Granma Internacional*, which has been published since 1996 and has an Italian translation that can be viewed online on a daily basis, was not enough. No, it was necessary for the Italian communists to offer Fidel Castro's régime a new avenue for propaganda, as if it didn't already have enough.

This development verges on the absurd and it is shameful for a democratic party to be providing propaganda services to a dictatorship that is forcing Cubans to flee in whatever flies or float, in search of a better future.

Revolutionary Cinema or Propaganda Films?

Film production does not escape the list of methods used in Havana's attempts to influence public opinion. The Rome Festival could have served as a visiting card for Walter Veltroni111, a man who has accomplished positive and interesting works, and is also a genuine film buff. But when Goffredo Bettini, mayor Veltroni's right-hand man, organized the (2007) festival, he chose

---

[111] Born 1955. Italian writer, journalist, and politician; former mayor of Rome. [Editor's Note]

to insert a pro-Castro 3-day film marathon under the direction of the indispensable Gianni Minà. The festival did not screen true Cuban masterpieces like *Fresa y chocolate* (Strawberry and Chocolate), *Guantanamera* and *Lista de espera* (Waiting List), nor even David Riondino's amusing *Velocipedi ai Tropici* (Bicycles in the Tropics). Perhaps these films were too critical and free-spirited regarding the Revolution, shot by honest and inspiring filmmakers who came down hard on the mistakes and shortcomings of Cuban society. Instead, five apologetic documentaries by Minà were screened: Entrevista a Fidel (Interview with Fidel [1987]), El Papa en Cuba (The Pope in Cuba), Un día con Fidel (A Day with Fidel), Cuba, treinta años después (Cuba, Thirty Years Later), Castro relata a Guevara (Castro Chronicles Guevara) and a film devoted to Subcommander Marcos. To top it all, we had to listen to Minà state absurdities such as "This work of mine has endured years of embargo in Italy". I would like to know who produces Minà's films, uncritical as they are and devoted to a commander who has never had so much publicity. His documentary makes no mention of the Cubans prisoners of conscience listed by Amnesty International, who risk their lives every day in their struggle for freedom. As far as he's concerned, they don't exist.

Minà insists: "I wanted to tell the story of the island as it is today, from the inside, with the voices of the generation that will soon be governing the country," said Gianni Minà in reference to his two-part documentary Cuba en la época de Obama (Cuba in the Time of Obama), screened during the Filmmakers' Days—September 7 and 8, 2011—at the Venice Film Festival. A non-fiction film shot in 14 days on the Castro brothers' island, covering thousands of kilometers, from Havana to Guantanamo.

Minà is entitled to tell whatever story he wants in Cuba en la época de Obama; no one can deny him that. We live in a democracy, as opposed to Cuba, where only the authorized may speak and only those who agree with the régime's ideas are authorized to produce cultural works for dissemination on the island. The problem isn't so much Gianni Minà offering up the usual clichés about the country being under siege by the Empire, about Cubans in love with Fidel and firmly believing in the positive implications of the transfer of his power to Raúl, about the alleged direct democracy via a show of raised hands, about the evils of the embargo, about the fantastic state of health of Cubans, and education for all. The serious problem is the Venice Film Festival giving credence to propaganda documentaries sponsored by the Cuban government and aimed at showing the good side of a régime that stands against basic freedoms.

The real Cuba is described in the works of Guillermo Cabrera Infante (who died in exile in London), in the writings of Virgilio Piñera, in Reinaldo Arenas's deathbed autobiography *Antes que anochezca* (Before Night Falls), in the novels of Pedro Juan Gutiérrez and Leonardo Padura Fuentes (*La novela de mi vida* [The Story of My Life] and *El hombre que amaba a los perros* [The Man Who Loved Dogs]). There is no need for defenders of a régime in decline parroting Granma's opinions, calling Yoani Sánchez[112] mercenary and stigmatizing dissidents as people on the CIA's payroll. If the Venice Film Festival wanted to show a worthy film on Cuba shot by Italians, there was *Desideri su una stella cadente* –*Cuba nel cinquantesimo anniversario della Rivoluzione* (Wishes on a falling star – Cuba in the 50th year of the Revolution), made by three extraordinary Rai 3[113] journalists: Jacopo Cecconi, Paolo Cellammare and Giammarco Sicuro.

What Cubans need is not mystification, but realism. They know their world will inevitably change and that the generation that will guide the Cuba of tomorrow will have nothing to do with the Communist Party. Cuba needs to open itself up to the world and make civil rights a part of daily life; it needs freedom of

---

[112] Born 1975. Cuban blogger who has achieved international fame and multiple international awards for her portrayal of life in Cuba under its current government.

[113] RAI is Italy's public broadcasting service and largest television company. [Editor's Note]

movement, freedom of thought, of the press, economic freedom, tolerance and respect for the dignity of human beings. At the present moment, with all due respect to those Italians who monitor our politically correct thoughts, it lacks every one of those things.

The Role of Gianni Minà in the Character Assassination of Yoani Sánchez

Gianni Minà finally dealt with the Yoani Sánchez phenomenon by breaking two years of silence in order to define her contemptuously as a *trendy blogger*. Up until that time, he had confined himself to ignoring her. But when he realized that even Fidel Castro was forced to acknowledge her existence in order to refute her daily life stories, the Cuban dictatorship's loyal supporter felt called upon to enter the fray. Minà's opinions regarding the criticisms against this antidemocratic régime consist of cut-and-paste party news bulletins, official statistics, and rhetorical catchphrases. It is as if a drizzle of malicious rumors were raining down upon us, all aimed at making us understand that the Yoani Sánchez phenomenon is bogus, a construct of someone very high up.

Perhaps the young blogger became irksome ever since the publication of *Cuba libre – Vivir y escribir en La*

Habana[114]. Minà criticizes the Cuban writer, but he doesn't get into the literary content and the stories of daily life. As justification for his critique, he uses a letter from a regular reader of his own blog, who says it is not true that the blogger who challenges Castro is free of ideologies or political interests. He talks of a skillfully orchestrated media operation. Nothing could be more absurd.

For the past two years, Yoani Sánchez has been managing an incredibly popular blog that, for the first time since the days of Heberto Padilla[115], talks about Cuba in a way that is free of ideologies, portraying daily life and the difficulties of surviving in a world bereft of freedom and of hope for the future. Gianni Minà seems incapable of understanding this, and recites as if from memory a timeworn script consisting of set phrases literally taken from the columns of *Granma* or from *Cubavisión*'s news programs. Once again, he speaks of a continent asking that the embargo be lifted, and details Cuba's record regarding education, health,

---

[114] Published in Italian by Rizzoli as *Cuba libre. Vivere e scrivere all'Avana*, and in English by Melville House as *Havana Real*.

[115] 1932-2000. Cuban poet, activist, and later exile. Padilla came to international attention for a political scandal in revolutionary Cuba that is known as the "Padilla affair." (1971). [Editor's Note]

social welfare, culture, and athletics, and a senseless and unjust economic blockade.

Yoani Sánchez calls for the lifting of the embargo, but she knows perfectly well that the U.S. economic blockade is not her country's only problem, merely one of them. Some others are things Cuban youths yearn for, strange objects called freedom of speech, of movement, of the press, of expression, of thought, even of economic freedom, without fear of saying something "blasphemous". Cuba's young people would like to see the end of an absurd monetary system that pays wages in Cuban pesos, in a country where basic goods are purchased with false currency, the convertible peso (with an artificial exchange rate equal to or even higher than the US dollar).

Gianni Minà states that Sánchez is unknown in Cuba. In all probability this is true. Who is going to speak of Yoani Sánchez when the press, TV, and radio are owned by the state and directed by the Ideological Department of the only political party legally existing, which has also been in power for half a century? Does Gianni Minà actually believe that anyone inside Cuba, which has one of the worst access rates to the Internet in the world, can read Yoani Sánchez's blog? In Cuba, where publishing houses are also owned by the state, not a lot is known of the complete works of Reinaldo

211

Arenas, Cabrera Infante, Zoé Valdés, Pedro Juan Gutiérrez, nor Abilio Estévez, Cuban writers all appreciated throughout the free world, yet marginalized in their own homeland, where censorship prevents the public from accessing all of their writings.

In an attempt to implement the character assassination of Yoani, Gianni Minà continues to tell the usual conspiracy theory of dissidents being financed by the CIA and being in cahoots with international terrorists. With that goal, he resorts to anecdotes that he doesn't hesitate to twist in convenient ways in order to support his assertions. He wants to make us believe that three poor afro-Cubans—who in a desperate attempt to escape the island tried to hijack a passenger boat in 2003, and without having harmed anyone were shot to death within a week—were dangerous terrorists[116].

I have been translating Yoani Sanchez's blog since its early days, when hardly anyone knew about it. I've always believed in her and am among those who wanted to have her book published by an important Italian publishing house. I know for a fact that everything arises in her spontaneously and unbidden, to

---

[116] Lorenzo Copello Castillo, Bárbaro Sevilla García, and Jorge Luíz Martínez Isaad hijacked a boat on April 2, 2003, to leave the country, and were captured the following day, then executed by firing squad eight days later, on April 11. [Editor's Note]

give life to the voices of the streets, to allow the hidden Cuba to speak, through a true personal exorcism that enables a young female blogger to personify the silent protest coursing through the island. My translations have always been voluntary. It is not the CIA's money that generates them. Everyone is fed up with that declamation. Money is of no use in telling the truth; the only thing of use in order to tell the truth in a dictatorship is a hefty dose of courage. What use can money have if you are accused of crimes against the security of the state and sentenced to capital punishment or to rot in prison?

The Italian journalist, Fidel's friend, also gave *L'Unità* a hard time, finding it guilty of paying too much attention to Yoani Sánchez. He argues that if a right-wing journal such as *Internazionale* reproduces Yoani's articles it is evidence of her ideological affiliation to their politics (even if her work is also reproduced by a much different type of paper such as Spain's *El Pais*). The Cuban government uses everything in its power to counter any attempt to describe the real face of Cuba, beyond its political games and the rhetoric of the government.

Minà does not allot even one minute of his time to mentioning that Cuba is a country with no freedom of the press, where there is only one correct (and allowed) way to think, and freedom of movement is nonexistent. He doesn't say that Cubans survive thanks to remittances sent by emigrants, especially those living in the hated Miami. No, Minà would rather vilify Yoani and write that she and all the other bloggers who talk about the shortages of everyday necessities are creatures of the Prisa media group (publisher of *El País* in Spain and owner of the news website *Noticias 24* in Venezuela). He goes on to say, without the slightest hesitation, that Yoani was "launched" to center stage by the Prisa media group, of which *El Pais* is a member.

It is striking that Gianni Minà launched an attack against *Wired* when it devoted twelve pages to Yoani Sánchez, and also against *Il Fatto Quotidiano* when it launched an appeal in support of Yoani. He dismisses *La Stampa*, which devotes a daily column to Sánchez on its Home Page and reports on her opinions in their print edition.

When Minà lashes out at *Wired*, he described Yoani as a creature of little credibility on the run from government bad guys who won't allow her to go pick up all the awards she has received all over the world from organizations hostile to the revolution. Yoani has received invitations from the Turin Book Fair, Columbia University, Internazionale, and the Pisa Book

Fair… Are they all imperialist groups hostile to the revolution?

Minà's rhetoric is aimed at assassinating the reputation of a person as hard to delegitimize as Yoani Sanchez, a blogger that uses narratives of daily life as her best weapon. A writer that tells the problems of a society deprived of the highest human possession: freedom.

Yoani Sánchez is such an authentic character that she should need no defending against an unknown like Salim Lamrani or a minor celebrity like Gianni Minà, but since she cannot leave Cuba because the régime won't allow it, I will take the liberty of speaking in her defense, though my right to reply is not welcome by her accusers.

It is worth noting that the option of adding comments has been deactivated on both *Latinoamerica*'s website and on Gianni Minà's own blog, something that neither the Italian nor Spanish version of Yoani Sanchez's blog prohibits[117]. This is almost as if to say that the only real version of the truth is that which the former websites' authors claim to be authentic. They

---

[117] One may access the Italian version at the following address: **www.lastampa.it/generaciony** And the Spanish version here: **http://www.desdecuba.com/generaciony/**

do not allow any duplication of their entries, either, in pure Castroist style.

Minà makes the claim, with an almost sinister tone, that "Yoani transmits from Havana with the aid of a German server (owned by the tycoon Josef Biechele), with a bandwidth 60 times greater than any used in Cuba."[118] But the truth is that Yoani transmits from Havana via email; her posts are published online by Spanish contributors because she cannot access the blog. She can't see it; she's a blind blogger.

She explained the situation herself in an interview:

Cuban citizens cannot run a business and buy a web domain for private or collective use; much less purchase a domain abroad to host on a national server. In Cuba, obtaining an internet address is the exclusive privilege of state institutions — not even authorized projects, if they are alternative, have access to such luxuries.

This is why if a citizen aspires to be a webmaster, he or she must ask people living in another part of the world for help in order to build a website. In mid-2006, we decided to ask our friend Josef Biechele if he would do us

---

[118] The bandwidth in Cuba is the second worst on the planet after Mayotte according to the 2010 Annual Akamai Technologie Inc, so it does not matter if the server was located in Berlin or Haiti, either would have more and better interconnectivity than Cuba. [Editor's Note]

the favor of buying the domain desdecuba.com.[119]

Josef was born and raised in Germany, but he is one of our best friends; we've known him since the nineties, when he visited Havana. We became great friends despite our different points of view on certain political and ideological topics. Malicious people have accused Josef of belonging to the CIA, but the only true thing is that in his youth our friend was an active communist party member, and to a large extent he still retains his ideals. Josef knew about my interest in information technology and immediately came to my aid when I had the idea of acquiring a domain in Germany. He used his name to have it hosted on the server of the German company Strato, and helped us with the initial investment, which was just over forty Euros per year. It was a significant sum relative to Cuba's low wages, but we would have two years of breathing space, paid for by him, to save up for the next installment.

Would anyone ask the CIA for 40 Euros a year to create a blog? I believe this explanation by Yoani is enough to respond to those insinuations.

Useless Ambushes

Yoani is constantly being followed by undercover State Security agents. Any serious journalist who has had the good will to interview her can verify this. Salim Lamrani, on the other hand, a little known freelance

---

[119] http://www.desdeCuba.com.

journalist that writes on Internet sites ideologically close to the Cuban Government's position, was able to interview the blogger without any difficulty. After obtaining the interview, the usual propagandist tricks, used to enhance Lamrani's thesis, were played out.

Minà claims that "Salim Lamrani, a researcher and professor at the University of Paris Descartes, easily located her and talked for hours at the lobby of the Plaza Hotel" It is true that he met and spoke with her, but he then wrote what the government deemed convenient. It is also true that he did not have any difficulty in meeting up with her and holding the interview, because the difficulties are provided by the Cuban government not by Yoani, who belongs to a generation that expects to persuade other through reason, while living though the hardships of daily life.

Salim Lamrani's interview was published and translated by *Latinoamerica*. A magazine that never bothered to publish an article by Yoani but which, on the other hand, gave plenty of space to an obviously trumped-up interview. If there is a tape recording, let's hear it because it's unthinkable that a real interviewer would ask such very long questions and that a brilliant and well-educated young woman such as Yoani would answer only yes or no. I know Yoani Sánchez very well, and I know that she's not the same person that's described in this made-up interview.

The "Gunmen" in Action

To be fair, the Cuban shooting squads for character assassinations have not limited themselves to attacking Yoani Sanchez. Gianni Minà has also attacked *Corriere della Sera*, criticizing it for having turned against Cuba after the death of the detainee Orlando Zapata[120] as a result of his hunger strike. Take note: he doesn't describe Zapata as what he was, he doesn't say he was a political prisoner fighting for human rights; rather, he defines him as *a detainee,* as per the government's slant that wanted to portray Zapata and Guillermo Fariñas[121] as common criminals, not as individuals fighting for their freedom.

Gianni Minà is astonished that the Italian press, (*Corriere della Sera* was not alone in appealing for human rights in Cuba), should pretend to adopt positions regarding the Cuban situation; and to further bolster his arguments, he states that there are worse situations

---

[120] 1967-2010. Cuban mason, plumber, political activist, and prisoner who died after fasting for more than 80 days. [Editor's Note]

[121] Guillermo Fariñas (b. 1962), Cuban psychologist, independent journalist, and political dissident. He has conducted 23 hunger strikes over the years and been jailed three times for a total of 11 years. He was awarded the Sakharov Prize in 2010. [Editor's Note]

in the southern parts of the world that nobody is concerned about. True, but we're talking about Cuba, and for Cubans, that is logically their first priority. We're talking about a divided people, who are forced to become expatriates if they migrate, or who live with the thought of escape constantly on their minds because they can't survive in their homeland and are deprived of freedom. It is haphazard to assume that the voices that have been raised to tell the world what is happening in Cuba are part of a campaign against Cuba. Gianni Minà cannot speak of an *anti-Cuba campaign* because there is no such organized campaign; there are only free voices talking about what goes on in Cuba. Let's not confuse the régime's character assassination practices–inside and outside of Cuba–with the voices of the people.

The Cuban-style reputation-killing firing squad is the most common in Italy and very similar to *Granma*'s: saying without saying, projecting shadows onto those who tell the truth about Cuba, quickly dis-authorizing their voices as either acting on behalf of the imperialists or in all likelihood paid directly by the CIA and working in collaboration with the United States government. They insist that the *Damas de Blanco* (Ladies in

White)[122] are purported to be financed by terrorists. For them, the only innocents are the Cubans in positions of authority, the gerontocracy in power who, for the good of the people defends them against Cuba's enemies. Never is a mistake or failing admitted; the answer to every problem that arises is always: "The embargo is to blame for everything." Were it not for the embargo, Cuba would be a thriving, prosperous and free country. Everyone would be living happily, singing hymns to Fidel and Raúl during mass rallies in Revolution Square. It's amazing how reality can be twisted around. Despite their acknowledgement of what they describe as "internal tensions", these collaborators of a foreign dictatorship know little or nothing about how Cubans live, exhausted by more than fifty years of dictatorship, their hopes betrayed by a revolution they all wished for and believed in. In 1959 no one wanted Batista jus as today many are fed up with the Castro family and a dictatorship that prevents free thinking.

The Italian "gunmen" assume the right to attack Sánchez, calling her a manufactured dissident while stirring hate against the critics of the Cuban régime, and claiming that those alleged dissidents are murky

---

[122] *Damas de Blanco* (Ladies in White) is the name that has been given to all of the protesting mothers, daughters, and spouses of political prisoners. [Editor's Note]

figures on the United States' payroll. They choose to forget that in 2010, Zapata Tamayo died as a result of a hunger strike and that Guillermo Fariñas was going down the same path. What mercenary has ever died in a hunger strike? For these people, it is unbelievable that pockets of dissent exist in Cuba, that people are tired that the same group of *gerontócratas* are still in power, presiding over an economic and social disaster that the embargo cannot be accounted for all by itself, even though it has played out as the primary alibi of Cuban leaders to justify their poor performance.

The real media campaign is not against Cuba, in the sense of its dictatorial régime, but against this farce, of which the newspaper *Granma*, Cuban television, and foreign "gunmen" are part. Yoani Sánchez frightens the people in power because she talks about everyday life in Cuba without raising her voice.

The régime represents the conservative position, not the revolutionary or progressive ones. It is the never-ending repetition of worn-out dogmas that have been overcome by history. The régime's foreign propagandists and watchdogs are called upon by that reactionary gerontocracy to battle on their behalf. Part of their current job is to assassinate the reputation of a young blogger that represents the future. This is understandable, because due to autonomous citizen initiatives such as the blog *Generation Y,* a true revolution may finally born, but this time understood as a movement towards changes that bring about freedom and the triumph of prosperity.

DIGITAL
Granma
INTERNACIONAL

CIREN
Centro Internacional de Restauración Neurológica

| ESPAÑOL | ENGLISH | FRANÇAIS | PORTUGUÊS | DEUTSCH | | Solo Testo |

• CUBA
• NUESTRA
  AMERICA
• ESTERI
• SPORT
• CULTURA
• ECONOMIA
• SCIENZE E
  TECNOLOGIA
• TURISMO

COMUNICATE
CON I
CINQUE EROI

• RIFLESSIONI FIDEL

L'OPINIONE GRAFICA

SPECIALI IE GI

• **Fino alla
  Vittoria Sempre**
  Sito Web di Ernesto
  CHE Guevara
• **120 YEARS' CLUB**

• A GIRO DI POSTA
  avuelta@granmai.cip.cu

ESTERI

L'Avana. 26 Aprile 2010

Cosa c'è dietro la nuova campagna contro Cuba

• Articolo di Gianni Minà apparso sul Fatto Quotidiano con il titolo: "La mia Cuba tra verità, complotti e falsi dissidenti"

Caro Direttore,

approfitto della tua disponibilità a ospitare voci fuori dal coro per riflettere su un tema, Cuba, che mi appassiona e che conosco in profondità. Da dieci anni, infatti, dirigo la rivista Latinoamerica, con l'aiuto di scrittori, poeti e premi Nobel di una parte di mondo che sta cambiando pelle e che per questo in Europa è spesso raccontata con pregiudizio.

Il Corriere della Sera, ad esempio, per tre volte in due settimane, con le firme di Pierluigi Battista, Elisabetta Rosaspina e Angelo Panebianco, si duole che la campagna scatenata recentemente contro Cuba dopo la morte del detenuto Orlando Zapata in seguito ad uno sciopero della fame, non abbia suscitato un coinvolgimento dell'opinione pubblica italiana, e in pratica chiede sanzioni. L'accanimento del Corriere della Sera è singolare, specie considerando che il giornale più diffuso d'Italia ignori, nello stesso tempo, notizie inquietanti sull'America latina (la mattanza di giornalisti in Messico con 15 morti quest'anno o 12 l'anno precedente, o il ritrovamento in Colombia della più grande fossa comune del Sudamerica con duemila vittime) mentre non dà requie a Cuba. E' iniziata evidentemente una campagna alla quale non si sottrae nessuno e che a volte sfiora il grottesco.

Wired, per esempio, è una rivista patinata delle edizioni Condé Nast, interessata ai nuovi media e alle nuove tecnologie. Nell'ultimo numero dell'edizione italiana ci sono una dozzina di pagine su Yoani Sanchez, bloguera di moda per la quale si è speso con un appello anche Il Fatto Quotidiano. Lanciata dal gruppo Prisa, quello di El País, Yoani trasmette dall'Avana aiutata da un server tedesco (di proprietà del magnate Josef Biechele) con un'ampiezza di banda 60 volte più grande di qualunque altra utilizzata a Cuba. Su Wired Yoani viene fotografata e raccontata come un'improbabile modella in fuga dai cattivoni del governo, che non le danno il visto per andare a ritirare tutti i premi che le vengono assegnati in mezzo mondo da organizzazioni ostili alla Rivoluzione. La povera bloguera è costretta a dare appuntamenti ai giornalisti occidentali alle dieci del mattino al Parque Central.

Yoani Sánchez is described as "fashion blogger, launched by the Prisa Group" in the newspaper *Granma International*.

Yoani Sanchez is defined as "cibermercenaria" in EcuRed, the Cuban Wikipedia. "Anyone who utters a criticism is immediately branded as a terrorist or traitor, as criminal or amoral." Yoani has expressed in her blog *Generation Y*.

"Common criminals" Post by Yoani Sánchez in her blog Generation Y, on January 21, 2012

Common criminals

Post by Yoani Sánchez in her blog Generation Y,
on January 21, 2012

To the memory of Wilman Villar Mendoza[123]

A couple of years ago, my friend Eugenio Leal decided ask for the report of his criminal record, necessary paperwork when applying for certain jobs. With confidence, he applied for the form where it would say he had never been convicted of any crime but found, in its place, a disagreeable surprise: it appeared that he was the perpetrator of a "robbery with force" in the town where he'd been born, although in fact he had never even run a red light. Eugenio protested, because he knew this wasn't a bureaucratic error nor a mere accident. His activities as a dissident had already made him the victim of repudiation rallies, arrests and threats, and now a blot on his criminal record had been added. He had gone from being a member of the opposition to someone with a past as a "common criminal," something very useful to the political police to discredit him.

---

[123] Wilmar Villar Mendoza, 31 years old dissident who died on January 20, 2012 in Cuba, due to the effects of a hunger strike of 56 days [Editor's Note]

If we allow ourselves to be guided by government propaganda, there is not a single decent person on this island, concerned about the nation's destiny and who hasn't committed crimes, who is also against the system. Anyone who utters a criticism is immediately branded as a terrorist or traitor, as criminal or amoral. Accusations difficult to "disprove" in a country where, every day, the majority of citizens have to commit several illegalities to survive. We are 11 million common criminals, whose misdeeds range from buying milk on the black market to having a satellite dish. Fugitives from a criminal code that strangles us, fugitives from "everything is forbidden," escapees from a prison that starts with the Constitution of the Republic itself. We are a population almost imprisoned, in the expectation that the magnifying glass of power hovers over us, raking through our lives and discovering the latest offense.

Now, with the death of Wilman Villar Mendoza, once again the old system of State insult repeats itself. A note in the newspaper *Granma* described him as a common criminal, and perhaps soon there will be a TV program —Stalinist style— introducing the alleged victims of his abuses. The objective is to minimize the political impact of the death of this 31-year-old citizen, convicted in November of contempt, assault and resistance. The official propaganda will attempt to downplay the importance of his hunger strike and shower his name with all sorts of derogatory adjectives. We will also see the testimony —violating the Hippocratic oath— of the doctors who attended him and probably even his mother will come out against her deceased son. All this, because the Cuban government can't permit even a glimmer of doubt in the minds of ordinary TV viewers. It would be very dangerous if people started to believe that a regime opponent would sacrifice his life for a cause, to be a good patriot and even a decent man.

ABOUT THE AUTHORS

Ramon Guillermo Aveledo

 Doctor in Political Science. Lawyer, politician, professor and prominent Venezuelan intellectual. He is the author of eighteen books on legal, political and historical themes. He writes a column for *Globovision, El Impulso, El Nuevo País, Notitarde y Meridiano.*

He was a deputy in the Congress of the Republic of Venezuela for the Lara State for three constitutional terms. He was also the head of the parliamentary Social Christian fraction in Congress and twice President of the Chamber of Deputies. During the presidency of Luis Herrera Campins he was Private Secretary to the President. He also served as President of Venezolana de Television from 1983 to 1984.

Rafael Rojas

 Historian and essayist. Studied philosophy at the University of Havana and history at the Colegio de México. He has lived in Mexico City since 1991, where he is a professor and researcher at the Center for Economic Research and Teaching (*Centro de Investigación y Docencia Económicas,* CIDE) and contributes to the magazines *Vuelta, Nexos, Historia Mexicana, Encuentro de la Cultura Cubana* and *Apuntes Posmodernos.* He is the author of several books and won the Isabel Polanco Essay Prize in 2009 for "*Repúblicas de aire: utopia y desencanto en la revolución de Hispanoamérica*".

Uva de Aragón

Writer, journalist, professor. Assistant Director of the Cuban Research Institute (CRI) at Florida International University (FIU) from 1995 to 2011. Associate Editor of the academic journal *Cuban Studies* from 1998 to 2003. Has written a dozen books the most notable of which include the essay collections *Crónicas de la República de Cuba 1902-1958* (2009) and *Morir de exilio* (2009); the essays *El caimán ante el espejo: Un ensayo de interpretación de lo cubano* (1993) and *Alfonso Hernández-Catá: Un escritor cubano, salmatino y universal* (1996); and the novel *Memoria del silencio* (2002). She writes a weekly column for the newspaper *Diario de las Américas*. As an expert on Cuban topics, she is often quoted in the press in different parts of the world. She obtained her Ph.D. from the University of Miami.

Juan Antonio Blanco

 Historian and political analyst. Graduated with a degree in philosophy from the University of Havana and has a doctorate in the History of International Relations. In Cuba, he was a founding member of the National Commission for the Issuing of Scientific Degrees in History. He was a university philosophy professor, a foreign policy analyst, and a diplomat for the Cuban government at the United Nations. In 1992 he resigned from his governmental positions and founded the Félix Varela Center in Cuba, an institution exclusively funded by international NGOs from the OXFAM family, that he directed until moving to Ottawa in 1997.

In Canada he was the global coordinator of the world human rights conference Vienna plus Five in 1998 and then later elected Executive Director of Human Rights Internet. He is also a consultant since 2004 to regional networks of Latin American and Caribbean Afro-descendants. From 2010 to 2012 he was the Visiting Associate Director of the Cuban Research Institute at Florida International University. In 2012 Dr. Blanco was the coordinator for the production of an academic white paper on the "Cuban Diaspora in the XXI Century" that he also co-authored and was broadly published.

He is currently the Executive Director of the Center for Latin American and Caribbean Initiatives at Miami Dade College. Dr. Blanco has given numerous conferences in universities and think tanks such as the Council of Foreign Relations and has published articles and essays in several specialized journals in the Americas and Europe. He is the author of the book *Tercer Milenio* (1994, 1995, 1998, 1999).

Ana Julia Faya

Political analyst and consultant. A graduate of the School of Arts and Letters and of the Instructors Course of the Department of Philosophy at the University of Havana. In Cuba, she was Assistant Researcher at the Center for American Studies (*Centro de Estudios sobre América*, CEA); guest professor at the Higher Institute for International Relations (*Instituto Superior de Relaciones Internacionales*, ISRI) and at the University of Havana; an officer of the Americas Department of the Central Committee of the Cuban Communist Party; editor and researcher at the Council of State's Office of Publications; and editor-in-chief at several publishing houses. In Canada, she has worked with the Canadian Foundation for the Americas (FOCAL) and as a consultant on programs about Cuba.

She has published the book *El despliegue de un conflicto* (1979) and written numerous articles about Cuba and the Latin American and Caribbean regions for publications in the United States, Spain, Canada and Latin America. She currently resides in Cornwall, Ontario, Canada.

Carlos Alberto Montaner

 One of the most widely-read journalists in the Spanish-speaking world. The magazine *Poder* estimated at 6 million the number of readers who on a weekly basis read his columns and articles, published in dozens of newspapers and magazines.

He has written some 25 books of essays and narratives. In 2007, he received the "Tolerance Prize" awarded by the Autonomous Community of Madrid, and in 2010 the "Juan de Mariana Prize in Defense of Freedom", awarded annually by the Juan de Mariana Institute. He divides his time between Madrid and Miami.

Gordiano Lupi

Writer, essayist, translator, and journalist for *La Stampa* of Turin. He is a translator for Alejandro Torreguitart Ruiz, Yoani Sánchez, William Navarrete, Félix Luis Viera, Heberto Padilla, and other Cuban writers.

An essayist specialized in Cuba and Italy in regards to themes of literature, film, and politics, with over 12 published works.

An established blog author: *Being educated for free*, on Cuba, (www.gordianol.blogspot.com) and *The Caino Cinematheque*, dedicated to Guillermo Cabrera Infante.(http://cinetecadicaino.blogspot.com/).

Among his most prominent works are the following: **Nero tropicale** (Il Foglio, 2000) –Cuban tales, **Orrori tropicali** (Il Foglio, 2002) –tales of horror, **Cuba Magica** (Mursia, 2003) –essay about Santería, **Un'isola a passo di son** (Bastogi, 2004) –on Cuban music, **Almeno il pane Fidel-Cuba quotidiana** (Stampa Alternativa, 2006) –on the "special period" and daily Cuban life, **Mi**

Cuba (Mediane, 2008) –photo essay on Cuba, **Fellini - A cinema greatmaster** (Mediane, 2009), **Sangue Habanero** (Eumeswil, 2009) –Cuban thriller, **Una terribile eredità** (Perdisa, 2009) –Cuban thriller, **Per conoscere Yoani Sánchez** (Il Foglio, 2010) –biography on the Cuban blogger, **Fidel Castro – biografia non autorizzata** (A.Car, 2010) –life and works of a dictator. This last book won Lupi the Tuscan Writer of the Year Award (*Premio Scrittore Toscano dell'Anno*) in 2011.

INDEX

A

Allard, Jean-Guy, 187, 195
Allen, Luis, 123
Álvarez Tabío, Pedro, 39
Andrew, Christopher, 18
Andropov, Yuri, 18
Arenas, Reinaldo, 208, 212
Arias, Desiderio, 77
Aveledo, Ramón Guillermo, 3, 4, 11, 31

B

Balaguer, Joaquín, 153
Barletta, Amadeo, 26, 76, 77, 78, 79, 80, 81, 82, 83, 84, 86, 87, 90, 95, 96, 97, 98, 99, 100, 101, 102, 103, 104, 105, 106, 107, 108, 109, 111, 112, 113, 114, 115, 118, 119, 121, 122, 123, 124, 125, 126, 127, 128, 129, 132, 133, 137, 139, 142, 145, 146, 147, 148, 149, 151, 153, 154, 155
Batista, Fulgencio, 26, 41, 42, 43, 44, 54, 56, 58, 59, 63, 64, 65, 66, 82, 89, 91, 98, 99, 100, 106, 107, 109, 115, 119, 134, 137, 145, 146, 148, 161, 164, 177, 183, 185, 221
Battisti, Amleto, 128, 129

Betancourt, Luis Adrián, 65, 66
Bettini, Goffredo, 205
Bisbé, Manuel, 100
Blanco, Juan Antonio, 3, 4, 11, 33, 75, 234
Blanco, Katiushka, 39
Bosch, Juan, 101

C

Cabrera Infante, Guillermo, 207, 212, 238
Carrión Obeso, Alfredo, 185
Casielles, Jaime, 120, 121, 122, 123, 124, 125, 126, 127
Castro, Fidel, 23, 26, 27, 39, 41, 42, 43, 44, 45, 48, 54, 55, 58, 59, 61, 66, 67, 82, 92, 93, 105, 115, 146, 159, 160, 162, 163, 164, 165, 167, 171, 174, 175, 176, 177, 183, 201, 205, 206, 207, 209, 213, 221, 238, 239
Castro, Raúl, 27, 163, 168
Cecconi, Jacopo, 208
Cellammare, Paolo, 208
Chibás, Eduardo, 42, 60, 61, 68, 161
Churchill, Winston, 97

Cirules, Enrique, 103, 104, 105, 106, 107, 111, 113, 114, 115, 116, 117, 118, 119, 120, 121, 122, 123, 124, 125, 126, 127, 130, 131, 133, 134, 135, 136, 137, 138, 139, 140, 141, 142
Collazo, Rosendo, 57
Conte Agüero, Luis, 183
Cortina, José Manuel, 68

D

Dalton, Roque, 29
Damas de Blanco, 22, 220, 221
Davidovich, Lev, 7
de Aragón, Ernesto R., 61
de Aragón, Uva, 3, 4, 11, 24, 25, 51, 233
de Armas, Ramón, 47
Deitche, Scott M., 105, 108, 109, 116
Diliberto, Oliviero, 204
Dorticós, Osvaldo, 161, 163

E

English, T. J., 104, 105, 119, 141
Estévez, Abilio, 212

F

Fariñas, Guillermo, 22, 219, 222
Faya, Ana Julia, 3, 4, 11, 27, 29, 157, 236
Fernández Retamar, Roberto, 47
Fernández, Marta, 106
Franqui, Carlos, 48, 163, 164, 171
Freisler, Roland, 9
Fujimori, Alberto, 10

G

Galeano, Eduardo, 47
García, Alfredo, 182
Ginjauma Montaner, José de Jesús, 183
Giuliano, Maurizio, 168, 169
Goebbels, Paul Joseph, 9, 179
Gómez, José Miguel, 45
Gómez, Máximo, 166
Gramsci, Antonio, 160
Grau San Martín, Ramón, 41, 44, 60, 63
Guevara, Ernesto Che, 58, 165
Guiteras, Antonio, 41, 161
Gutiérrez, Pedro Juan, 208, 212

H

Hart Dávalos, Armando, 68
Hart, Herbert L. A., 35
Hornedo, Alfredo, 68

I

Ibarra, Jorge, 47, 59

K

Karol, K. S., 30
Kelsen, Hans, 35

L

Lacey, Robert, 108, 109, 110, 116, 144
Lamrani, Salim, 215, 217, 218
Lansky, Meyer, 108, 110, 118, 120, 121, 124, 128, 144
Latsis, Latvian M. I., 94
Le Riverend, Julio, 47

Lechuga, Carlos, 100
Lenin, Vladimir Ilich, 10, 94, 159
Lewis, Oscar, 30
Lobo, Julio, 91, 92, 123, 124
López Segrera, Francisco, 47
López Vilaboy, José, 106
Lupi, Gordiano, 3, 4, 11, 31,
    197, 238

M

Machado, Gerardo, 41, 42, 53,
    68
Madoff, Bernard, 132
Márquez Sterling, Carlos, 25,
    26, 44, 51, 58, 59, 60, 61,
    62, 63, 64, 65, 66, 68, 69,
    71, 72, 73
Marrero, Leví, 51, 137
Martí, José, 40, 41, 42, 45, 47,
    166, 174
Martínez Estrada, Ezequiel, 47
Marx, Karl, 161
Masó, Calixto, 51
Matos, Huber, 48, 176
Mella, Julio Antonio, 41
Minà, Gianni, 200, 201, 206,
    207, 209, 210, 211, 212,
    213, 214, 215, 216, 218,
    219, 220
Mitrokhin, Vasili, 18
Montaner, Carlos Alberto, 3, 4,
    11, 27, 28, 173, 193, 195,
    237
Montesinos, Vladimir Lenin, 10
Moreno Fraginals, Manuel R.,
    104
Musolino, Maurizio, 204
Mussolini, Benito, 76, 95, 96,
    97, 105, 125, 126, 127, 154

N

Navea, Felipe, 57
Núñez Portuondo, Emilio, 68

O

Obama, Barack, 76, 207
Ochoa, Arnaldo, 115
Ortega, Gregorio, 105, 126, 127

P

Pacino, Al, 24, 83
Padrón, José Luis, 65, 66
Padrón, Pedro Luis, 102
Padura, Leonardo, 7, 208
Pérez, Louis, 135
Pérez-Lanzac, Carmen, 190
Piñeiro, Manuel, 167
Piñera, Virgilio, 208
Pino Santos, Oscar, 47
Pinochet, Augusto, 18, 23
Prío Socarrás, Carlos, 41, 60
Puzo, Mario, 103, 118

R

Ramonet, Ignacio, 40, 41, 42,
    43, 48
Rivero Agüero, Andrés, 61
Rivero Agüero, Nicolás, 57
Roa, Raúl, 78, 100
Roca, Blas, 68
Rodríguez Iturbe, José, 7, 8
Rodríguez, Pedro Pablo, 47
Rodríguez, Rolando, 39
Rojas, Rafael, 3, 4, 11, 24, 25,
    35, 39, 232
Roosevelt, Franklin D., 76

S

Sáenz Rovner, Eduardo, 111, 130, 134, 135
Sakharov, Andrei, 18, 22, 23, 192, 219
Salvador, David, 164
Sánchez Arango, Aureliano, 60, 61
Sánchez, Celia, 162, 166, 167
Sánchez, Yoani, 29, 195, 208, 209, 210, 211, 213, 214, 215, 218, 222, 238, 239
Sanguily, Manuel, 45
Sartre, Jean Paul, 47
Schmill, Ulises, 36, 37
Schmitt, Carl, 36
Sicuro, Giammarco, 208
Sloan Jr, Alfred P., 133
Solzhenitsyn, Aleksandr, 9, 192
Soto, Lionel, 47
Stalin, Joseph, 7, 8, 9

T

Torreguitart Ruiz, Alejandro, 200, 238
Trafficante, Santo, 105, 108
Trotsky, Leon, 7, 8, 160
Trujillo, Rafael Leonidas, 10, 76, 77, 78, 79, 80, 101, 146, 148, 154

U

Urrutia, Manuel, 48

V

Valdés, Zoé, 212
Varela, Félix, 161, 234
Vargas Llosa, Mario, 10
Vásquez, Horacio, 101
Vega, Aníbal, 57
Vega, Víctor, 57
Villar Mendoza, Wilman, 227, 228
Vitier, Cintio, 47

W

Wilson, Gordon, 108
Wright Mills, Charles, 47

X

Xiaobo, Liu, 70

Z

Zapata, Orlando, 22, 219, 222
Zelaya, Manuel, 76

15281670R10130

Made in the USA
Charleston, SC
27 October 2012